Money Wealth

and

Prosperity

Money Wealth

and

Prosperity

Using Self-Hypnosis to Get It

Tawan Chester PhD, MhypD

Dumouriez Publishing

Jacksonville, Florida

Money Wealth and Prosperity: Using Self-Hypnosis for a Better Life

Warning:

Self-hypnotic recordings should never be played whilst driving or at any other time when you need to maintain a full awakened state of consciousness.

Published by:
Dumouriez Publishing
P.O.Box 12849
Jacksonville, Florida 32209

Copyright ©
Tawan Chester
All rights reserved.

This copyright covers materials written expressly for this volume. Reproduction or transmission by any means, electronic or mechanical, including photocopying and recording, or by information storage or retrieval system, with the exception of brief quotations in reviews or articles must be arranged with the individual copyright holder.

ISBN: 0-9764387-7-1
ISBN13: 978-0-9764387-7-9

Dedication

This work is dedicated to those willing to take the reigns and control not only the money, wealth, and prosperity they experience but their destiny as well.

Contents

Dedication	....	9
Part I		
1. Getting Started	....	15
2. The Constants	....	19
3. Most Valuable Real Estate	....	23
4. Prioritizing Process	....	27
5. The Way to Success	....	37
6. Money	....	41
7. Wealth	....	43
8. Prosperity	....	47
9. Our Theory	....	51
Part II		
10. Recording Instructions	....	55
11. Listening Instructions	....	57
12. Types of Scripts	....	61
13. Parts of Scripts	....	65
14. Assembling Scripts	....	73
Part III		
Section 1 Opener	....	77
Section 2 Color Script A	....	81
Section 3 Inductions	....	87
Section 4 Color Script B	....	127

Section 5	Suggestions	133
Section 6	Color Script C	205
Section 7	Closer	213
Appendix	....	217
Index	....	219

PART I

Chapter One
Getting Started

The information presented here follows many of the techniques and methods of regular hypnosis and NLP. It is being presented in such a way that allows you to use them in a personal manner. You have been bombarded by subtle and aggressive programming your entire life. I feel if anyone is programming or hypnotizing you it should be YOU. Now no one is saying that they are programming you but that is what they are doing.

Many people shy away from the words programming and hypnotizing but the facts are there if you analyze them. With that in mind I have stuck with omitting them as much as possible and used the word recordings. Unfortunately, the programming most people use on themselves is negative and results in a high failure rate and low self-esteem. Hypnosis can be very helpful but I tend to trust the Self Hypnosis more. That is because so many factors are at play especially motives and trust. When you are the one controlling all of the main factors those things are not an issue.

You are told what to think, how to think, and at times when to think. It is high time you take the reigns and do your own programming. Your investment will be minimal but it can potentially produce maximum results. Some terminology has been removed because it is not necessary for our purposes. My colleagues and I are currently using these techniques and information but it is a substantial difference in cost than the price o this book.

I have discovered through my practices a few ways to utilize the regular techniques in a different way which tends to accelerate the individual's success. By making what this method available in this manner you are able to take advantage of my findings and help yourself in a wide range of areas. The most common subject areas are being presented here but you can make small changes in order to personalize them. Using the templates and information provided here you can assemble and make personalized recordings using your computer, digital recorder, cell phone, tablet, or other device. Digital recordings like Mp3s or Mp4s can be placed on a CD or electronic device and set to play continuously.

I have also had remarkable success using these techniques with my grandchildren therefore I have provided information that allows you to use these with your children or grandchildren. One of the best ways to build self-esteem is to program your inner voice with positive information. This is true no matter what age the individual is. The information presented is not just affirmations but techniques and methods that are simple but effective. The average individual may hear an equal of amount of positive and negative information during a day but for some reason society has geared them towards the negative. The negative information is therefore more likely to be noticed by them and take precedence in their lives. You can take charge of your life in a different way and affect the outcome of your daily life and the goals you set.

Einstein's theory of Relativity $E=mc^2$ states: Energy and mass are equivalent and transmutable.

Simply put:
Everything is related to energy and everything is interchangeable.

The General Theory of Relativity demonstrates that time is linked, or related, to matter and space, and thus the dimensions of time, space, and matter constitute what we would call a continuum. They must come into being at precisely the same instant. Time itself cannot exist in the absence of matter and space.

It is from this standpoint that we choose to take action. That means we allow what we do in one place to affect matter and space in all places because they are linked, they are relatively equal. We can change one substance into another as in alchemy because they are transmutable.

Everything is relative even your point of view. Day in and day out you move from a particular point. You are merely using what you were taught. The world uses the principles and knowledge that was handed down by those in power as acceptable.

The philosophical, scientific, mathematical, etc information we have come to know is accepted and used until someone else steps outside of the norm and explores the vastness of whatever else is out there. Oftentimes they're thought of as quacks, lunatics, dreamers, strange, etc until what they say brings results are is examined by others and found to be relevant. I often wonder how much material has been ignored or thrown to the wayside but could have also proved relevant and useful. Do you dare to discover the untapped uncharted regions that are around you? If you do, continue on because you have just made an investment in the right thing.

There is an old proverbial saying that says:

> *A butterfly flapping its wings in the one country can affect the weather in another country located on the opposite side of the world. (Paraphrase)*

Science has shown that whatever a person does today has the ability to affect the earth and those that come after him or her years or centuries later…This is known as a carbon footprint. That which is formed in the mind and fed with the thought energy will manifest in the physical realm. Everything that you see in the world is merely energy manifested in different forms.

Chapter Two

The Constants

There are few things in our world that appear to be a constant...These particular things happen whether you want them to or not. They are what they are and as occupants of this world, we must make adjustments accordingly. They occur like clockwork so to speak and try if you will but you cannot change them. In making adjustments in your life, you can anticipate their occurrence but you are not always prepared when they do. The times at which they do occur can be either a joyous occasion or a devastating one.

In the east, this is called Yin & Yang and in other places, it is simply looked at as Balance. All things must maintain balance to operate efficiently and optimally otherwise the scale is tipped and things move in a manner that could be destructive. These constants operate as they do because you cannot have one without the other. They are ever-present. When you are able to see one of them know that the other one is invisible, behind the scene helping to hold things together in their perspective place. This constant balancing action takes place all the time and in all things. It is prevalent in atoms, which are part of the basic makeup of everything.

This in not a complete list of constants but it will serve our purpose.

Ebb & Flow
Light & Dark
Hot & Cold
Positive & Negative
Seedtime & Harvest
Good & Evil
Attract & Repel
Life & Death

You can see the constant of Ebb & Flow being displayed by the oceans of the earth. The tides rise and then fall. Each wave that greets the shoreline stays long enough to quickly kiss and caress it then turns and rushes away as fast as it came. Wind, rain, or weather systems may affect the pace at which it occurs at but they will take place just the same.

Light & Dark share each day or year in some regions. The season of the year may appear to affect the amount that you see of each. It is actually the tilting and rotating of the Earth on its axis as it orbits the Sun. The strange thing about this constant is that it still maintains its balance. At the time an area maybe having longer periods of light during a day, there is an area that will be having longer periods of dark at the same time.

Most inhabitants of the Earth view Seedtime & Harvest as a time designated for food. This is usually the greatest concern when dealing with this constant. When planting for crops the seasons of the year, the area being seeded, and caring for what was planted are always major concerns.

This constant occurs in other veins that are not given much thought at all. It is called "mating season" when referring to the other inhabitants of the Earth but this is a constant for all inhabitants. I guess it just sounds better, feels better to the mind, and seems to place humans far above others on the evolutionary scale when humans use a different term when referring to themselves and mating. A quick look at the behavioral patterns of most humans and you will see there is really not much difference. I simply state that here for the purpose of helping you see things for what they are. So that you can take, charge and focus your thoughts in a manner that will be more beneficial to you.

Because humans are higher on the evolutionary chain, they are almost entirely responsible for the world that you see around you. Modernization, technology, civilization, etc is all the workings of humanity. Each and every thing big or small is part of a harvested seed that was planted at some point in time in the mind of someone. Buildings, automobiles, tools, etc all had to start with an idea. The idea had to be formed into a feasible plan. The workable plan had to be made that could be reproduced successfully into the finished product.

> *The idea (seed) came to the mind (planted), it was cared for (plans), over and over again making adjustments when need (revamping plans, blueprints, calling in experts, researching), watching/tending to it while it was being built/formed (growing), completion of the project or invention for the world to*

The fact is we are constantly harvesting the thoughts that we plant (big or small), and care for. We can check our thoughts by examining what is in our world. You immediate world around you is the sum total of your thoughts. Your actions are derived from your thoughts. When someone does something outrageous or something that goes against the morals or the society in which they live, others will often ask, "What were you thinking?"

In order to reap a harvest you must sow seeds. You are always either sowing seeds or caring for seeds that you have planted. Your seeds are ideas. You care for those ideas with thoughts and actions.

Chapter Three
Most Valuable Real Estate

An old saying years ago was:

Where the head leads the tail will follow.

This puzzled me for years. I finally got up enough nerves to question what it meant. This is what I was told...When you see a dog or other animal going somewhere you see it going headfirst. No matter where that head goes its tail is going to follow it. That made a lot of sense and it also applies to humans as well. We just do not have tails that wag. Really though I understood it to mean: If your mind has said you are going somewhere or doing something your entire body must go along with it.

Our purpose here is to take charge of a very important area. It may very well be the most important area in the world. In fact, I believe it is the most valuable piece real estate on the planet. It is however, often overlooked, ignore and used as a dumping ground. This is the area in which people do all of their planting in...It is a field of dreams...It is your planning board…It is you very own wishing well…Your personal pot of gold…Your Fairy Godmother…It is your mind.

The most uncharted untapped territory in the universe and it is at your command. It is your mind. When I speak of the mind I am referring to all levels of it (conscious, subconscious, higher conscious, super conscious, etc).

The problem you have with getting the money, wealth, and prosperity that you want is not with the mind itself. The problem lies with the commands that you are constantly giving to it. It follows each and every one of your commands to the letter. It does not take into account the true relevance of them or the danger to you because it takes each command seriously.

The subjects of money, wealth, and prosperity are addressed here because at times they are so tightly intertwined and connected. They are also used interchangeably by many people. Other than the subject of love or food they are the most common concerns of humans. Oftentimes, it is said that if you possess money, wealth, or prosperity then they in turn will get you love or food.

Reaching Your Goals

There are many factors that contribute to the outcome of any given situation. When working towards any goal you want to not only know what these factors are but you will need to know how to control them. It is necessary that you know what has the greatest influence on you being able to achieve your goals.

It is essential to find out what foundational tools you need to start any endeavor you undertake and lean how to identify what could slow you down or interfere with your momentum so that you can be successful sooner than later. You also want to identify things that could hinder your progress, cause setbacks, or knock you off track when you are trying to reach your goals.
By taking charge of your command center and feeding it the right information at the right time you are on your way to great success.

It is said that humans utilize approximately 10 percent of their brain. That is quite shocking to know. It makes one feel somewhat lazy. The fact is up until now we appear to know only one way to use our brain. A more correct statement maybe that we have chosen to only use our brains one-way. We have heard of and seen other ways but we have chosen to dismiss them.

Chapter Four
Prioritizing Process

It does however prioritize all of your commands. It rates the importance of a command based on the amount of thought and energy you give to each. The more thought and energy you give to a command the more important it is and the higher up the list of commands it is placed.

Whether something is good for you or bad for you is never an issue or factor when the mind prioritizes a command. There are things that you can do to influence the way the mind prioritizes commands and ultimately what it manifests and the order in which it manifests things for you. Your knowledge and understanding of things along with how they work will influence the commands. Your emotions and fears will also affect the process as well.

The one that will factor in the most will be the one that poses the greatest push or pull on the emotions or fears. Certain stressors are dangerous to a person's health but they trivialize them and learn to live with them to the point that disease appears in the body. In many cases, if they would consider all things and minimized the stress the disease may not have occurred.

In the mind, nothing is ever negated but everything is prioritized. It prioritizes everything then it is either pushed forward until it manifests or held back until the right time comes to manifest it. If the right time never comes then the thing is never manifested.

Here is an example of what happens in the mind.

>Scenario One:
>You say, "I need to get a raise."
>Command to brain, "Get a raise."

The mind has translated that statement into a command to get a raise. It then allows the thoughts to race towards fulfilling that command. This will involve assessing, planning and actions you can take to make that happen.

The mind makes an assessment of as many different things as it can for you to do…ask someone else for advice, ask the boss for a raise, increase my education, network, increase my productivity, and be more visible…

It then maps out a plan and moves forward putting those plans into action.

This is with just one command so nothing needs to be prioritized. Now we add another command.

Scenario Two:

>You say, "I need to get a raise."
>Command to brain, "Get a raise."

The mind has translated that statement into a command to get a raise. It then allows the thoughts to race towards fulfilling that command. This will involve assessing, planning and actions you can take to make that happen.

The mind makes an assessment of as many different things as it can for you to do…ask someone else for advice, ask the boss for a raise, increase my education, network, increase my productivity, and be more visible…

It then maps out a plan and moves forward putting those plans into action.

You now add a second command to the brain.

>You say, "I want a new car."
>Command to brain, "Get a new car."

The process starts all over again.

You have given two commands to the mind. It must now prioritize them.

The brain's prioritizing mechanism now kicks in and it looks to prioritize so it considers what you said. You gave it two commands and they contained the words, "need and want."

This process uses information and understanding to sort out the two commands.

A NEED means necessity (usually ranked with life sustaining)
A WANT means emotional gratification

That was easy huh? Well it does get more complicated so we will go on. This is the basic processing route that the mind takes but it gets more complicated when the other factors start to influence things. They tend to make manifesting quite difficult because they are allowed to run ramped and unchecked. If controlled and used wisely they can prove advantageous to your efforts.

Scenario Three

> You say, "I need to get a raise."
> Command to brain, "Get a raise."

The mind has translated that statement into a command to get a raise. It then allows the thoughts to race towards fulfilling that command. This will involve assessing; planning and actions you can take to make getting a raise happen.

The mind makes an assessment of as many different things as it can for you to do…ask someone else for advice, ask the boss for a raise, increase my education, network, increase my productivity, and be more visible…

It then maps out a plan and moves forward putting those plans into action.

You add a second command to the brain.

> You say, "I want a new car."
> Command to brain, "Get a new car."

The process to make it happen (getting the car), now starts all over again.

You now add a third command to the brain.

> You say, "I really need a new suit."
> The process to make it happen (getting a new suit),
> starts all over again.

You have given three commands to the mind and it must now prioritize them.

Once it receives information the brain then looks to prioritize so it considers what you said. You gave it three commands and they contained the words, "need and want."

<u>It again uses information and understanding to sort things out.</u>
A NEED means necessity (usually ranked with life sustaining)
A WANT means emotional gratification

Remember from the last scenario a need is considered top priority in most minds so that goes to the top of the list. The problem now is that two of your commands contain the word need. The command with want is again pushed to the bottom of the list. The mind now goes to the other factors to help it prioritize the two commands that contain the word need.

<u>The mind now looks to emotions and fears</u>
There are several different ways to rationalize the two but ultimately it will all be how it weighs in the mind of the individual.

Raise and suit are both needed
Raise…to get new suit and other things
New suit is easy to get then work on raise and the new suit may even help me get the raise

Whatever is decided upon the mind will work to push it into manifestation. The two with the need, the raise, and the new suit will take up the first and second positions on the list with the car coming in last.

Outcome 1:
1. Raise
2. New suit
3. New car

Outcome 2:
1. New suit
2. Raise
3. New car

A NEED:
is considered top priority in most minds so it goes to the top of the list.

This is a simple and yet basic demonstration of how the mind processes the commands that you give it. There is however, the unchecked factor that is allowed to run ramped through the mind. The problem that all have but very few face it or do anything about it. It is the thoughts that are used to fuel the commands.

Let us look at the earlier scenarios. The person decided in scenario number three to prioritize. He or she wanted to end up with outcome number one. Then he or she would want to keep fueling the mind with every thought that will keep him or her moving towards getting the raise first. If the car manifests before the raise or new suit does then it would make sense that the individual may have been fueling the mind with negative thoughts concerning the raise and new suit but positive ones concerning the car.

Here are some sample statements that would cause the mind to shift and reprioritize the list of commands.

The boss is a jerk.
I'll never get a raise with the kind of boss that I have.
They'll only give me an insignificant amount as a raise and it wouldn't be worth my time.
My boss doesn't like me.
They don't like to pay you what you're worth on this job.
They give the new people the high pay so there's nothing left for giving the rest of us a raise.
No matter what I do I can get a raise or get ahead.
I can easily get a new suit but it'll take forever to get a raise.
They think that I can't get nice things without a raise.
They're trying to keep me down.
They think they can have nice the but no one else can.
I'll show them.
They can try to stop me but I'll get a new suit and new car some way.

Commands containing statements such as the follow examples will be placed at the bottom of the list of priorities. When these types of statements are made, it tends to tell the brain they are impossible to achieve in this lifetime. These are more or less daydreaming reference points and are not to be worked on or use until the individual wants to waste time.

It would be nice to have…

I sure wouldn't mind being…

If I had…

If I could…

One day I might…

A NEED:
is consider top priority in most minds so it goes to the top of the list.

Chapter Five

The Way to Success

Many of the activities, actions, affirmations, spoken declarations, etc presented here may seem pointless, a bit silly, or even stupid boarding on the idiotic. They all work together and serve our purpose. Their main purpose is to get you where you need to be so that you can accomplish your goals life concerning money, wealth, and prosperity. These are focusing tools because they help us focus or maintain our focus.

Certain things must line up in your mind, body, and spirit (that is where the focusing comes in). These things must be as one and the must flow in a constant synchronized manner with the world around you. No "ifs, ands, or buts," about it. They must be as one, remain as one, and continually flow in you are to reach your goals without any setbacks.

There are many factors that contribute to the outcome of any given situation. The factor that carries the most weight is what is in the mind…Your mind. Most of the factors influencing a situation either fall under your control or are somehow influenced by you. It is important that you find out what factors are involved in every situation and then act accordingly. Be sure to always make adjustments if and when needed because nothing is really engraved in stone.

Things can be changed in other words and you should not hesitate when a change is needed. Do not act rash or in haste but gather the information needed and continue gathering information and checking your progress. Simply put you should research thoroughly before advancing. You are always at liberty to make adjustments to your actions in order to get the most out of every situation.

I found that out first hand when I started looking for a home to retire in. Property after property manifested in the price range that I had stated. So what was the problem? What should I say needs to be adjusted? The problem was that I had not thoroughly researched and gathered all the information that I should have. I had to make some serious adjustments and I mean quick. I had a list that I was using for what the new home had to have but on the fly, I added waterfront to my list. Wouldn't you know it, a property appeared. Two stories nestled on a one and a half acre lot with a nice creek running down one side (nice and private it was).

I did not like the feel of the ground when I walked the property so I made some adjustments to my thought commands. I knew that I did not want to be near a marsh or a creek but rather a lake, a river or a beach. I also added a pool to my list at that point that I felt would be good for exercising, family use, and entertaining. Now, I knew about pool upkeep and maintenance costs so that was considered before I added that to my list. Well almost as soon as I added those changes to my list (within two days), several properties popped up.

In looking at the properties that came up these are what I had to pick from. One house was excessively close to the water's edge for me. One home was rather high up but had a beautiful flight of stairs leading down to the water. One had neighbors that were way too close with no fence in between. Another one was located at the end of an unpaved road with a private lake that was shared with only one other home. The last home could be considered perfect but had a tax assessment that was five thousand dollars more than any of the others. After viewing the last home, I halted the search until I made a more detailed specific list.

Some of these I chalked up as "been there, done that, and don't want to do it again." I learned my lesson and therefore I am passing that information on to the next person. The setback was not a harsh one and can be viewed as very minor but it did require that I adjust my momentum and stop my forward motion. Every person is different and what works for one may not work for another but the information here concerning a detailed specific list and the mind is what I found to be basic. It is so basic that it can be used as a foundational building block for everyone.

Things to Avoid

Here are a few things you want to avoid and even eliminate because they will be counterproductive to you or cause major set backs in your plans.

Despair

Becoming Hopeless

Becoming Unfocused

Getting off Track

Selfish

Being Anxious

Giving Up

Doubting

Not completing what you start

Canceling out what you have done

Negativity (thoughts, words, emotions)

Stopping the flow of good energy

Going back to old ways

Do whatever you need to in order to eliminate these from your thoughts. I have found it useful to throw myself into full celebration mode when any thought concerning a projected goal comes up. Fully throwing oneself into celebration mode tells your mind and the Universe that you have accepted the fact that you have gotten what you wanted and you are happy about it. It leaves not room or time for negative thoughts concerning your goals.

Chapter Six
Money

The old saying, "Money is the root of all evil" is one of the biggest falsehoods ever. It is a misquotation from Holy Writings.

For the love of money is the root of all evil…I Tim 6:10a kjv

In fact, it has been so grossly misstated that it can be said that the statement is an outright lie that has kept many people miserable.

Looking at to another sacred writing by one who was thought to be one of the wisest men to walk the earth King Solomon we must view money in a different way. According to this particular passage taken from the same Holy Bible money is actually the answer to everything…Yes, your read that correctly.

A feast is made for laughter, and wine maketh merry: but money answereth all things. Eccl 10:19 kjv

It is a known fact that if you do not possess the right key for a specific door, you will never be able to unlock it. It is high time you did away with the little things that keep you from reaching your goals. Here we work with you to help you identify and use the right key for the right door. That right key is the mind…Once that is on track everything else has a better chance of falling in place.

Money is in fact a currency and it is meant to flow like an electrical current. Oftentimes we try to catch and hold it in only one form. The form of money we are most familiar with is the legal currency of a country. Many things have been used as an item of exchange especially when parties are bartering for goods or services. You may want to take that into consideration when you are looking to increase in the area of money.

Chapter Seven
Wealth

Wealth is not something that can be obtained overnight. It is a copulation of teachings, thoughts, and actions that move you into a state of being. It is a state wherein the mind has been well trained. The wealthy thoughts continuously flow through the mind to spark wealthy actions.

Every thing produces after its own kind…Every action that is fueled by a wealthy thought produces a product of that thought. The manifestation of large amounts of money is merely a by-product of a wealthy mentally.

A wealthy state of being produces planned actions that seemingly ensure success. The physical manifestation of wealth may take years to appear or it may show up overnight. Whichever way it manifests it still remains the product of the teachings, thoughts, and actions concerning money.

A Wealth Filled Mind

In order to be a person with a wealthy mind existing in a wealthy state of being, you really must have a wealth-filled mind. Your mind can formulate hundreds to thousands of thoughts a day. If the ones concerning money are formed in the right way, they will cause a manifestation of money to appear in large quantities.

The neurotransmitters in the brain fire extremely fast and look similar to lightning. These firings move here and there throughout the brain and across the great divide of the brain. They are responsible for the brain being able to process all data that the body receives.

When your mind produces thoughts concerning wealth they must be accompanied by actions of wealth if you are going to manifest wealth. The thoughts that flow through your mind fuel your actions and push you towards wealth.

One thing that individuals living in a state of constant lack do is curse those that have wealth. This I must say is a very big mistake. When the individual cursing those with wealth just because they have it, he/she is actually sowing seeds of discord and laying a trap that backfires. It throws things out of the round so to speak. It can even disrupt the natural ebb & flow of things.

Unfortunately, the harvest of seeds of "Ill will" may do one of two things. The harvest of those seeds maybe just right for the picking when the individual obtains some semblance of wealth, then it affects him/her. The harvest of those seeds can appear to be wild vines or weeds that continually hinder the individual's progress towards obtaining wealth by providing obstacles. It will always benefit one to sow seeds of "Good will or Blessings" so that when the harvest comes back to him/her it will be beneficial.

Wealth Actions

It is best to "mark the perfect man" so to speak. That is take note of the person occupying that state you would like to obtain or be in. Then imitate his/her actions to obtain a like state of being. Model closely after someone (in thought & action), that has gone before you and has accomplished what you aspire to accomplish.

You are becoming a mentee from a distant. It is not necessary to become a fanatic but find out as much as you can about what they did and how they did it. Once you obtain that information, you should cater it to your style thereby making it a tailor-made plan. Wealth can be viewed as merely a bridge that conveys you from point A (money), to point B (prosperity).

The Earth is filled with an abundant supply of all things and there is more than enough for all to enjoy.

Wealth is not just having tons of money, loads of money, or an abundant supply of money. Wealth is not having control over a great deal of money but much much more. It is also a state of being, a state where there is absolutely no lack. Wealth also has the ability to serve as a very important bridge to move you into a much better position. It affords you a way of life that dreams are made of. Wealth is not something that can be obtained overnight but is a copulation of several factors. Anyone can obtain wealth if he or she knows how.

You can use a variety of system models to help create a viable plan that will move you into a wealthy place. There is a simple method that can be easily integrated with your style to create a workable plan that will help you reach a wealthy state. You must use a specific method or combination of methods when formulating your plans to achieve wealth. Using this method will help you move with great ease while executing your plans. The plans you make must be workable for you if you are to reach your goals concerning wealth.

Ask yourself these questions when setting goals or evaluating your progress:
- Are you placing obstacles in your path?
- Is what you are doing helping or hindering your progress?
- What type of harvest are you planting seeds for?

Chapter Eight
Prosperity

Prosperity is a state of Abundance. It is all around you in varying degrees. Prosperity can be spotted without using much effort if you know what to look for. Strangely, enough is that it can be hard for some to recognize. This maybe because what makes one person happy may result in misery for another.

Although there are many routes that can be taken to reach the state of prosperity you really, only need to take one. Some people can only see prosperity as it pertains to others. They cannot for the life of them see it in their own lives.

Being able to recognize abundance in your own life is extremely important. This knowledge helps you to prioritize the focus of your attention. This means that not every area gets the same focused attention. Some areas require direct focused action while other areas only need minimal focused attention. When an area requires direct focused attention it means that, the element of lack is present. This element prevents abundance from flowing because it is the direct opposite of it.

When it comes to direct opposites only one of them can be dominant in their appearance. When an area requires minimal focused attention it means that, the element of abundance is present. The focused attention requires is minimal to maintain the state. Everything requires some type of focused attention, energy, and action in keeping with the seedtime and harvest principle. It is important to be able to identify what type of attention best suits the situation.

Having crossed the void using the bridge called wealth, you are able to enter into a land that some legends say, "Flows with Milk and Honey." This is a place where there always is more than enough. There is an abundance of everything, around every single corner, and in every crack and crevice.

Prosperity involves a combination of several different things. What I have seen is that it like many other things is the result of teachings, beliefs, and actions. Many have entered into this state but took different routes to reach it. The main objective is to reach the goal of prosperity, by remaining open, focused, and diligent. By using as many available things as possible, you can create a state of abundance in a timely manner. Once the abundance is achieved in an area then continue in what was used to help maintain the desired state.

There are many that have achieved abundance in some areas but not all. They may have obtained a great abundance of money but lacked abundance in the areas of love, family, friendship, etc. Some have an abundance of love but deal with lack in the many other areas. To achieve the state of prosperity there will need to be abundance in the other areas as well. There must be a balance if one is to be prosperous and possess abundance in all areas. The state of prosperity can be attached to all things in life that contribute to an individual's happiness. It includes but is not limited to the areas of money, family, and love.

As beauty is in the eye of the beholder, Prosperity is in the mind of the beholder.

Chapter Nine
Our Theory

The theory behind our method is that your ears never stop listening and your brain never stops processing information. With that in mind know that you can receive information while you sleep. This is a key feature to the system that we have put together. If you are in a deep sleep, your subconscious will openly receive the suggestions and you will see quicker results.

Your natural state of sleep provides you with the very best atmosphere to program yourself. You are taking charge and choosing what goes into your mind. You are hypnotizing yourself for the things or life that you want. The world around you is constantly giving you suggestions whether you want them or not with this method you can choose what takes precedence.

It is easier to feed information to your subconscious while your conscious (waking mind) is not bossing you around. Using this method allows you to bypass your conscious mind and go straight to the subconscious mind while you sleep. If you do this when you are awake but in a restful relaxed state you will still have the conscious mind interfere when it wants to and that means it will take longer for you to see results. We use nonintrusive and nonaggressive methods to help you help yourself.

With any of our recordings that we use we recommend that the individual listens to the recording before putting it to use so that he or she is comfortable with what is being said. If you are comfortable with what is being said then you will be more willing to accept what is said. Therefore you want to completely ready through all the material contained within this book before making your own recordings. The recordings you make using this material are meant to reverse the negative programming and comments that have come into your environment over the years. They are intended to help reshaped your thoughts and actions to bring positive changes into your life.

The things that have lain in your conscious and subconscious mind have directed all of your actions. With you make recordings using the method and information presented here we are in essence working together, to replace negative programming with positive constructive programming. Your recordings will be working to bring about the results that you want in a timely manner.

PART II

Chapter Ten

Recording Instructions

The overall steps for making your recordings are as follows:
1. Select the type of recording you want.
2. Find the script template in the Appendix section.
3. Select the Suggestions you want to use.
4. Assemble your script using one of the easy to use templates.
5. Read the entire script aloud a few times.
6. Record on an available device such as a cell phone, tablet, IPod, computer, recorder, etc.
7. Listen to your personalize recordings.

To get the best results I suggest that you listen to the recording as many times as you need to quickly take on the new thoughts. The rule of thumb is for you to listen to each recording at least twice a day for the first 21-30 days. The best time to listen to a regular script is when you are not rushed but have time to relax. They are more effective when you listen to them in a relaxed state.

The script information provided allows you to make several different types of recordings. You can make recordings to listen to like music, to listen to while in a relaxing position, and to listen to while you sleep. The recordings can be made short or long. Some scripts can be made time specific so listen to them at the appropriate time (day or bedtime). For example, if the recording is for sleep then you want to listen to it just before going to sleep.

Results vary from person to person and situation to situation. Unless otherwise stated do not listen to any of the recordings while operating a motor vehicle or equipment where your full attention is required. The Power Play scripts are for making recordings that can be used anytime during the day like regular music recordings. They are especially good to use on a break or during a commute.

It is important that you have a hand in personalizing the recordings because it helps strengthen the points you are trying to make. There are several things working together to help you reach your goals in the shortest possible time. Commit to working with the information presented in a positive manner and you will be on your way to the success you seek.

Once you have assembled your script and read it a few times you may want to do a practice recording. When you have finished recording your script listen to it in its entirety so that you can check for errors. You want to make sure to speak clearly, slowly but steady when recording. The final recording needs to be as error free as possible. The smallest recording flaws can cause aggravation when you are programming. Remember you will be listening to these recording over and over. It is well worth it to practice reading the script before recording and to check it for flaws.

Chapter Eleven
Listening Instructions

Volume

The volume that you use when listening to any script is vital to your success. The volume must be loud enough to be effective but not so loud that the brain drowns it out. During the daytime or normal waking hours the world around you is quite busy and noisy.

You will need to set the listening volume at a level that drowns out the world around you while allowing you to feel comfortable. If the volume is too loud the brain will think it is noise and act to drown it out. You do not want that to happen because you are trying to get the brain to receive the information that you are hearing. If using a regular script then you are also trying to move into a deeply relaxed position. Noise will only irritate you and produce tension which may lead to insomnia.

At night most of the world around you has settled down or is asleep. There is less noise to contend with and therefore you can decrease your listening volume. When listening to a script while asleep, you want to keep the volume down extra low. If the volume of your player is up too loud it will cause you to come up out of your deep restful sleep. You get much faster results when you use a script while sleeping because the conscious mind is out of the way.

Listening while sleeping

This is a key part of our Self-Hypnosis system. It not only saves you time and money but it helps the overall process produce results in a shorter period of time. This technique was discovered by my colleagues and me 18 years ago. It is a very simple technique that works because your body works. It relies on your sense of hearing along with the ability of the brain to work without any effort on your part.

When using the Sleep recordings, turn the volume on your electronic listening device down really low, make adjustments if need. The volume needs to be low so that it doesn't startle you or disturb you while you are asleep Set the player on repeat so that you will hear the recording all night. Listen to the recordings every night for a few weeks. Make sure they are consecutive nights then change to every other day, then to once a week, then once a month. The time is shortened when you listen to the recordings at night so the time that is starts working varies.

One drawback to this method of listening while asleep is that it makes it difficult to listen to same recording when you are fully awake. That means for those that try to get double duty out of their recordings it cannot be done with these once the programming takes affect. It is worth it with these because you do get faster programming results using them. This is a way to check your progress when using this method. After approximately a week of listening to the recorded script at night try listening to it when you are fully awake. When the recording sounds like it is dragging you know it is working.

The overall programming has occurred quicker by listening to the recordings as the individual slept. This to me is the key to quicker reprogramming. I have used this method personally and professionally for years now with excellent results.

Listening while awake

When using a regular scripted recording sit or lie down in a quiet place where you will be undisturbed. Place yourself into a comfortable position—either sitting or lying, legs and feet uncrossed and slightly apart, hands resting loosely in your lap or by your side.

You want to make yourself as comfortable as possible. Place the volume at a comfortable level. Make sure that the volume is not so loud that it irritates the eardrums but loud enough to drown out any outside noises. Sit back, open your ears, and be receptive to all directions.

Please remember

When using the script while asleep keep the volume down extra low. If the volume of your player is up too loud it will cause you to come up out of your deep restful sleep.

When using the script while awake keep the volume at a comfortable level. If it is too high the mind will treat it like noise and attempt to drown it out. If the volume is too low then outside noises will interfere with your listening.

Only the Power recordings can be used at anytime of the day the other recordings must only be used when you are able to be in a relaxed situation.

Chapter Twelve

Types of Scripts

Three types of scripts can be assembled using the materials presented in this book. They are called Power Play, Awake, and Sleep scripts.

Power Play

Power Play scripts are used to make recordings that can be listened to at anytime of the day. They are the shortest scripts of the three but they can be just as effective. The Power Play recordings can be treated like music. They can be listened to while doing daily activities such as exercising and commuting. These have their own Opener and Closer. They are the only Opener and Closer that should be used when making the Power Play recordings.

It is because these recordings can be listened to like music any time of the day the other Openers and Closers should never be use with these. The regular Opener and Closer encourage the individual into different relaxed states which cannot always be done. Listening to these recording provides reinforcement to the other two types. It also makes for a type of quick listening programming. It does not mean that the programming itself will happen quickly but that the time required to listen is short and quick.

> For your ease and convenience templates have been placed in the Appendix section for you to use when assembling your script.

Awake Scripts

The Awake scripts are used to make recordings that can be listened to during the day but at a time when you are able to relax. They should never be listened to while you are driving, operating heavy machinery, or when you need to be fully alert. They are similar to a regular hypnosis session. The length of the recording can be increased by adding more suggestions. These provide a programming timeframe similar to normal hypnosis sessions.

Sleep Scripts

Sleep scripts are used to make recordings that can be listened to during the times that you sleep. Like the Awake recordings they should never be listened to while you are driving, operating heavy machinery, or when you need to be fully alert. These provide for the quickest programming and the highest level of influence when used as directed.

Your programming progress can be checked by listening to these during your waking hours. After you have followed the earlier instructions concerning listening to these recordings for about two consecutive weeks trying listening to one during your fully wakened state. Do not try to relax and use it as a programming session but listen to it like music. If it sounds like the words and sounds are dragging then you know the programming efforts with these are working.

Chapter Thirteen
Parts of the Script

Normal scripts for hypnosis can be quite long. Administering them to an individual can take even longer. The results are unpredictable as is the length of time it takes for it to become effective. The entire process can be quite costly and time consuming. When the results of hypnosis are positive and the targeted goals are reached it is priceless. I do believe if used properly the methods presented in this book can be beneficial you in several ways. It can help improve your confidence and self-esteem.

This method of self-hypnosis can also save you a lot of time and a great deal of money while helping you reach some very valuable goals concerning money, wealth, and prosperity. A script used for hypnosis can contain many parts that work together for a single purpose. We will use the minimum amount of parts to construct the scripts but they will still have the same affect. The scripts will be used with a few special techniques which will make them more effective than ordinary scripts alone and will prove to be more valuable to you.

Six parts are needed and five of them have been made available for use in the scripts that you will assemble. The parts you will be using are called Openers, Closers, Inductions, Color Scripts, Suggestions, and background sound. The scripts can be made without background sound but it is a very important part of the recording. Background sound is not being provided here because this is a book and because it is best that you pick the sound yourself.

The possible combinations for the use of the parts provided are numerous but we will only focus on making three types of scripts. One will be a short script that can be played anytime of the day like music. The two other scripts will be longer in length; one to be play when you are in a relaxed state and the other at night while you sleep.

It is important to note that the number of suggestions used in a script will dictate the length of the actual recording. You are able to assemble and use single or multi purpose scripts. I recommend you try both because they are useful and valuable. The multi purpose scripts are time savers because you are combining several different purposes in one recording.

The single script recordings contain only one purpose but can be lengthened by increasing the number of suggestions. That along with its other parts allow for quick listening. Therefore much like music recordings you can start and finish them quickly and on the go. Each individual part is simple but when combined forms a complex tools that is part of a dynamic system. Using all parts together is very important to the overall success and usefulness of the script.

Openers

What is normally called Lead-Ins in hypnosis is what we call Openers. They are used to lead the individual into a relaxed state so they are placed at the very beginning of the script. A relaxed state is always the state you want to be in before you start the main programming because it is a receptive state. The individual mind is more likely to accept the programming when done from this state. This is very important and therefore should not be overlooked.

You do not need to be asleep to be receptive and you do not have to be in a meditative situation either. Always make sure you are using the appropriate Opener and to assist you in this there are only two being presented here. They are the Power Play and Regular Openers. Make sure to only use the Power Play Opener when making recordings that will be listened to at anytime of the day. The regular Opener can be used for both the Awake and Sleep recordings. An Anchor or Trigger has been added to our regular Opener so that it has a dual purpose. Our goal is to use the minimum amount of time to receive the maximum amount of results.

Closers

Closers are used to end a session. They work to bring closure to what you are trying to do. The brain likes to have a starting and stopping point and this serves as that stopping point. We use three different types of Closers here to accommodate the time they the recording is being used. The Power Play Closers can be used for any time of day. The Awake Closers are for use when you have time to relax. When you are not operating a vehicle, heavy machinery, or need to be fully alert. The Sleep Closers are for recordings that will be used while you sleep.

Color Scripts (Triggers and Anchors)

Triggers and anchors are used to reinforce and solidify the programming. It is a way to get the most "Bang for your buck." It will help to keep your session working throughout the day and night. They are used as the word implies. When used triggers start an action or process when they are seen or heard. Anchors tie them into your mind and thoughts while giving them more weight (importance). Using these gives your recordings a boost of power.

I have found the best triggers and anchors are those that are simple and common. They have been combined and just called Color Scripts so as to save time and to help minimize the number of parts that need to be assembled in order to get a complete script. The simple ones require less thought and the common ones are so repetitive that they work for you as if on autopilot. You will use your effort to program the information and the world around you will help to reinforce it. The most popular colors were used in the Triggers (Color scripts) presented here so that you can use your favorite color.

You can substitute a color to suit your taste. Keep all of the words the same except the color. Aside from using your favorite color you can pick a color that you see a lot of. For instance if you are outdoors a lot you want to pick blue, green, or white. If you are in a wooded area then those colors would be brown and blue. You can pick flower colors too but the idea is to let a dominant color that you come in contact with often reinforce what you are doing.

Colors vary and so do the names for them so with that in mind you want to use the color name you are most familiar with. For instance, some use the color names turquoise, blue green, aquamarine interchangeably but for our purposes here it does not matter. The only thing that matters is what name you associate with a particular color.

Inductions

An induction is considered to be an act of bringing an individual into something or someplace. At times it is thought of as an introduction to or into something like and organization. Here we are giving it a twofold purpose. We are introducing you to something and using it as a deepener. The Inductions are worded in the form of a storyline to help ease you into the hypnosis experience so that it does not feel or seem like a boring or stiff session.

A deepener is used in hypnosis to get the individual to relax further and to become more open to receiving suggestions. This technique is very helpful when the individual needs to explore information stored at different levels, when the information tends to be deeply buried, or seemingly unknown.

Suggestions

The suggestions as they are being called here are similar to affirmations. The difference is the integration of NLP (Neuro-Linguistic Programming) techniques. Under normal circumstances when NLP wording is used you will find that it is very aggressive and fear filled. It is used in advertising and sales to get you to make purchases. It directs you to rush and purchase items before they are all gone or before an allotted time runs out. It also tries to describe products with words that wow the ears and make it sound like it is the best product in the world.

The wording used here is not aggressive but it has been kept moving in a certain positive matter of fact way. You have several different subjects to choose from when making your recordings. You can make single purpose or multi purpose recordings. The length of the recording will be longer if you increase the number of suggestions in each.

Specialized Suggestions

You can make your own specialized suggestions by following the wording you find in the Suggestion section. Keep these pointers in mind when making your own personalized suggestions.

- They must always be worded in a positive manner
- Keep them short and simple
- Only use words that stand for want you want or want to happen

Sample:

I make very good use of my time
Instead of
I do not waste time

You brain hears "waste time" and programs that action in causing you to do just the opposite of what you really want to do. It further emphasizes that because it may not like being told what not to do so it throws "do not" out of the window.

Samples:

I am a genius at playing the violin

I quickly learn all of my dance routines

I create very tasty food dishes

I am very successful at making beautiful craft items

Background Sounds

Background sound is a very important part of these recordings. It will help to relax you and occupy your thought process subtly. The sound can be instrumental (something you do not know the words to) but almost any classical low-key music will do if it does not have fast movements. The best background sounds are the nature sounds. Waves and oceans are the most relaxing followed by forest and birds. The sound should be low and should not over power your speaking voice. It is a background sound and it will help your mind focus by drowning out or lessening the noises in your environment.

Chapter Fourteen
Assembling Scripts

All of the parts of the scripts presented here are easy to assemble and make if you follow the templates provided in the Appendix section. You are to first select a category and the appropriate number of statements you would like. You can combine suggestions from the different areas when making your recordings. In other words all of the suggestions do not have to be from the same category. Several categories have been given for example test, confidence, business, etc. Each has been divided into a minimum of 10 statements. Ten being the smallest amount you want to use when making a recording.

Once you have decided on the number selections, just pick the template for the type of recording you want: Power Play, Awake, or Sleep. Then go to the sections listed on the template and pick the appropriate script for the type of recording you want to make. Follow the order of each part as it is listed on the template to assemble the full script to be recorded. Read the entire script aloud a few times before you begin to record it.

When you feel comfortable reading the script aloud you can then read it into a recording device while playing a background sound. Keep the background sound soft and low through the entire reading. It is a good idea to record a few seconds of the background sound before you start specking and after you finish reading the entire script.

When you finished listen to the entire recording. You want to make it as flawless as possible so take your time and speak clearly. You will have a recording that you can use right away. Recording it in your own voice helps to reinforce what you want and it also helps train you inner voice to speak positive things to you that will move you towards your goals.

Tips for making your recording:

- Read the completely assembled script aloud a few times before recording
- When reading the script maintain a low, quiet, slow but steady speaking voice
- Play a background sound while recording your script.

PART III

Section 1

Openers

Power Play Opener

> Power Play Opener is used when making scripts to be used at anytime of the day except sleeping. These are great for daily commutes, at lunch/break times, etc.

It is time to redirect the flow of thought into a new direction. These thoughts will be planted deep in my subconscious mind, take root and cause me to prosper. My conscious mind will remain alert and focus while my subconscious mind takes in all that is said and acts on it.

Each time I listen to this, it will be 10 times more effective in helping me reach my goals successfully.

Regular Opener

> This Opener can be used with any script that will be used when you have time to relax or meditate. **Never use with a power play script.**

I place myself in a very comfortable position, close my eyes, and begin inhaling deeply and exhaling slowly...

I continue inhaling deeply and exhaling slowly about five or six times...each time I exhale my whole body relaxes even more

Inhaling deeply...Exhaling slowly...

Inhaling deeply...Exhaling slowly...

I continue feeling calmer, more peaceful and more at ease...

Inhaling deeply...Exhaling slowly...

Inhaling deeply...Exhaling slowly...

As I continue relaxing, I will use my imagination...I will take in all that is said...

Inhaling deeply…Exhaling slowly…

It is time to let my conscious mind rest and my subconscious mind flow. It is time to redirect the flow of thoughts into a new direction which will be planted deep in my subconscious mind, take root and cause me to prosper. My subconscious mind will then synchronize with my conscious mind and move me into a more success and prosperous place. Each time I listen to this, it will be 10 times more effective in helping me reach my goals successfully.

Section 2
Color Scripts A

Aquamarine

Color Aquamarine Each and every time I see the color AQUAMARINE, whether consciously or unconsciously, my desire and determination to succeed will grow stronger. Each and every suggestion received in this session will work more and more effectively. I will not need to look for the color aquamarine, but I will just notice it automatically. It will be bright, sharp, and clear to me.

Black

Each and every time I see the color BLACK, whether consciously or subconsciously, my desire and determination to succeed will grow stronger. Each and every suggestion received in this session will work more and more effectively. I will not need to look for the color black, but I will just notice it automatically. It will be bright, sharp, and clear to me.

Blue

Each and every time I see the color BLUE, whether consciously or subconsciously, my desire and determination to succeed will grow stronger. Each and every suggestion received in this session will work more and more effectively. NOW, I will not need to look for the color blue, but I will just notice it automatically. It will be bright, sharp, and clear to me.

Brown

Each and every time I see the color BROWN, whether consciously or unconsciously, my desire and determination to succeed will grow stronger. Each and every suggestion received in this session will work more and more effectively. I will not need to look for the color brown, but I will just notice it automatically. It will be bright, sharp, and clear to me.

Fuchsia

Each and every time I see the color FUSHIA, whether consciously or subconsciously, my desire and determination to succeed will grow stronger. Each and every suggestion received in this session will work more and more effectively. I will not need to look for the color fuchsia, but I will just notice it automatically. It will be bright, sharp, and clear to me.

Gold

Each and every time I see the color GOLD, whether consciously or subconsciously, my desire and determination to succeed will grow stronger. Each and every suggestion received in this session will work more and more effectively. I will not need to look for the color gold, but I will just notice it automatically. It will be bright, sharp, and clear to me.

Green

Each and every time I see the color GREEN, whether consciously or subconsciously, my desire and determination to succeed will grow stronger. Each and every suggestion received in this session will work more and more effectively. I will not need to look for the color green, but I will just notice it automatically. It will be bright, sharp, and clear to me.

Grey

Each and every time I see the color GREY, whether consciously or subconsciously, my desire and determination to succeed will grow stronger. Each and every suggestion received in this session will work more and more effectively. I will not need to look for the color grey, but I will just notice it automatically. It will be bright, sharp, and clear to me.

Orange

Each and every time I see the color ORANGE, whether consciously or subconsciously, my desire and determination to succeed will grow stronger. Each and every suggestion received in this session will work more and more effectively. I will not need to look for the color orange, but I will just notice it automatically. It will be bright, sharp, and clear to me.

Pink

Each and every time I see the color PINK, whether consciously or subconsciously, my desire and determination to succeed will grow stronger. Each and every suggestion received in this session will work more and more effectively. NOW, I will not need to look for the color pink, but I will just notice it automatically. It will be bright, sharp, and clear to me.

Purple

Each and every time I see the color PURPLE, whether consciously or subconsciously, my desire and determination to succeed will grow stronger. Each and every suggestion received in this session will work more and more effectively. NOW, I will not need to look for the color purple, but I will just notice it automatically. It will be bright, sharp, and clear to me.

Red

Each and every time I see the color RED, whether consciously or subconsciously, my desire and determination to succeed will grow stronger. Each and every suggestion received in this session will work more and more effectively. .NOW, I will not need to look for the color red, but I will just notice it automatically. It will be bright, sharp, and clear to me.

Silver

Each and every time I see the color SILVER, whether consciously or subconsciously, my desire and determination to succeed will grow stronger. Each and every suggestion received in this session will work more and more effectively. NOW, I will not need to look for the color silver, but I will just notice it automatically. It will be bright, sharp, and clear to me.

Turquoise

Each and every time I see the color TURQUOISE, whether consciously or subconsciously, my desire and determination to succeed will grow stronger. Each and every suggestion received in this session will work more and more effectively. NOW, I will not need to look for the color turquoise, but I will just notice it automatically. It will be bright, sharp, and clear to me.

Violet

Each and every time I see the color VIOLET, whether consciously or subconsciously, my desire and determination to succeed will grow stronger. Each and every suggestion received in this session will work more and more effectively. NOW, I will not need to look for the color violet, but I will just notice it automatically. It will be bright, sharp, and clear to me.

White

Each and every time I see the color WHITE, whether consciously or subconsciously, my desire and determination to succeed will grow stronger. Each and every suggestion received in this session will work more and more effectively. NOW, I will not need to look for the color white, but I will just notice it automatically. It will be bright, sharp, and clear to me.

Yellow

Each and every time I see the color YELLOW, whether consciously or subconsciously, my desire and determination to succeed will grow stronger. Each and every suggestion received in this session will work more and more effectively. NOW, I will not need to look for the color YELLOW, but I will just notice it automatically. It will be bright, sharp, and clear to me.

Section 3

Inductions

> **Only use with Awake and Sleep scripts. Never use with a Power Play scripts.**

In this section you will find a variety of subject matter. Read them through and pick one that you like or it stands out. If one interests you then it will be of greater use to you. The wording does not follow the normal rules of grammar. Some words contain extra letters. In those instances you want to stress, elongate, or drag out that particular sound so that the word is longer than the normal.

The Candle

I imagine in my mind's eye a single candle which is lit. I focus my mind on the flame of the candle.

I notice the flickering and dancing of the flame.

As the flame moves I may see colors gently swirling around.

I may see reds, yellows, blues, purples, white, or maybe other colors.

I can see how beautiful the colors within the flames are. I keep the candle in my mind's eye as I go very gently and very deeply, into a profound state of relaxation.

As I keep the flame of the candle there in my mind's eye, the count will go down from 10 to 1.

Each number will make me 10 times more comfortable and more relaxed than I am now.

10 - 9 - 8 –deeper, deeper
7 - 6 - 5 relaxing more and more
4 - 3 - 2 deeply relaxed
1 - deeply, deeply relaxed…

I now notice the wax body of the candle and as I see the first trickle of melting wax begin to move down; I can become aware of the melting sensations within my peaceful body.

I now see the melting wax touch the candleholder and merge with it to become a part of the candleholder.

I am now very deeply relaxed and each and every suggestion will go deeply into my subconscious mind. I make them part of me.

I feel safe, comfortable, peaceful at ease, and deeply, deeply relaxed.

Countdown to Relaxation

In a moment I will count slowly backwards in my mind. I will count backwards from 10, and after each number I will think in my mind, the words, deeply, deeply, deeply relaxed. As I think those words in my mind, I will find that I become, deeply, deeply, deeply relaxed.

As I count slowly backwards in my mind, at any time I lose count or lose track, I will just start again at 10. Whilst I'm counting backwards with the conscious thinking mind, I'm going to be talking to the deepest part of myself, and I don't even need to consciously listen because my subconscious mind hears everything that needs to be heard.

At anytime I lose count, or lose track, I'll just start again at 10. I'll allow the suggestions to enter into the very deepest part of my mind, that wonderful place where those important changes in my life are taking place. The words will become my thoughts and my thoughts will generate a wonderful new way of being and feeling and thinking.

For now, I'll keep my mind focused on those numbers, counting slo-owly backwards from 10 to become deeply, deeply, deeply relaxed. Anytime I lose count or lose track, I will just start again at 10.

10…

Deeply, deeply, deeply relaxed…

9…

Deeply, deeply, deeply relaxed…

8…

Deeply, deeply, deeply relaxed…

I become more and more relaxed with every number that I count

7…

Deeply, deeply, deeply relaxed…

6…

Deeply, deeply, deeply relaxed…

5…

Deeply, deeply, deeply relaxed…

I am becoming more relaxed than I ever before

4…

Deeply, deeply, deeply relaxed…

3…
Deeply, deeply, deeply relaxed…

2…
Deeply, deeply, deeply relaxed…

I am comfortable and deeply, deeply, deeply relaxed

1…
Deeply, deeply, deeply relaxed…

I am in a state of deep and total relaxation

Crystal Cave

I imagine that I'm standing at the entrance of a very deep cave. Looking down I can see the entrance of the cave and it feels warm and inviting and safe.

Many steps lead deep down into the cave and I begin to walk down the steps, counting in my mind as I go down.

20 – 19 – 18 – 17 –16 – 15 – 14…I arrive at a small landing and walk across the landing to the next flight of steps. I notice that as I move down the stairs, I'm wrapped in a peaceful, calm, and inviting energy.
I continue down the next flight of stairs 13 – 12 – 11 – 10 - 9 – 8 – 7…I come to the next landing. This is a quiet peaceful place. There's a cool breeze blowing and I can see colorful lights dancing around the walls and a beautiful glowing light coming from the cave below. I walk over to the final flight of steps, counting again as I continue down 6 – 5 – 4 – 3 – 2 – 1. There's a warm inviting sensation here that beckons all who enter to come and enjoy.

Now I'm standing at the bottom of the steps. I walk forward into the cave and noticed at once where the colorful dancing lights came from. Hanging from the ceiling of the cave and on the walls are hundreds of different varieties of minerals. Red rubies, blue sapphires, and brilliant green emeralds adorn the walls of the cave; the light plays on the smoky quartz, beautiful citrines, and sparkling amethyst, displaying the beauty of the rose quartz and I can feel the energy coming from this wonderful mineral kingdom. (Pause). I feel peaceful, safe, and at one.

Dolphin Dreamtime

I imagine that I'm standing at the entrance of a very deep cave. Looking down I can see the entrance of the cave and it feels warm and inviting and safe.

Many steps lead deep down into the cave and I begin to walk down the steps, counting in my mind as I go down.

30 – 29 – 28 – 27 – 26 – 25 – 24 – 23 – 22 – 21 – 20 – I arrive at a small landing and walk across the landing to the next flight of steps. I notice that as I move down the stairs, I'm wrapped in a peaceful, calm, and inviting energy.

I continue down the next flight of stairs 19 – 18 – 17 – 16 – 15 – 14 – 13 – 12 – 11 – 10…I come to the next landing. This is a quiet peaceful place. There's a cool breeze blowing and I can see colorful lights dancing around the walls and a beautiful glowing light coming from the cave below. I walk over to the final flight of steps, counting again as I continue down 9 – 8 – 7 - 6 – 5 – 4 – 3 – 2 – 1. There's a warm inviting sensation here that beckons all who enter to come and enjoy.

I'm standing now at the bottom of the steps.

Looking deeper into the glowing part of the cave I see a narrowing where the way is lit with torches. I walk towards the light until I see more steps, leading deeper into the cave. I go carefully down – deeper down – to a deeper part of the cave – the lights grow brighter.

Treading carefully along the stony path I come to the end of the path. It leads out onto a small bay, and in the bay I can see the glistening bodies of playing dolphins.

I hear the beautiful inviting sounds of the dolphins and they call for me to join them. They move majestically and with such grace. I step down into the warm ocean. The dolphins teach me to swim playfully and carefree as they do. I feel at one with them. They take me deeper, deeper, and deeper down to the ocean's floor.

The dolphins show me their wonderful secrets. I know that I can return here and explore anytime that I'd like to. I have made wonderful friends for life. It is calm, peaceful, and serene here. This is a place of joy and harmony. It is a place to be playful and carefree. I feel at one moving in sync with the dolphins and with all of creation.

Flying Blanket

I imagine that I'm going on a picnic. I'm going with my favorite people to a special place for a picnic. I have all of my favorite things to eat and drink. I can see them. I can smell them. I can taste them.

I take time to enjoy and play games with my family or friends that have joined me on this picnic. When I'm finished eating and drinking and playing games, I glance over and see a blanket spread out on the ground.

This blanket is in my favorite color. It's smooth, soft, and comforting. I sit on it or lie on it. I feel that this is no ordinary blanket because it's a flying blanket and I'm the pilot. I'm in control. I can fly just a few inches above the ground, just above the grass, or even fly higher above the trees if I want. I'm the pilot.

I can go wherever I want to go and I can go as fast or as slow as I wish, just by thinking about it. I can do loop-d-loos or I can land and visit with my friends and family. I can land at the zoo, the beach or anywhere I'd like. I'm the pilot and I am in charge.

I might fly by a tree and see birds in a nest. I may fly to the top of a mountain or maybe to the end of a rainbow. I can speed up and slow down. I can just enjoy going where I want to go. I can take all the time I need to feel very comfortable. When I'm finish flying for the day I can find a nice, comfortable landing spot and land my flying blanket. Then I can just lay my blanket out under a nice shade tree and relax.
Relax…Relax…Relax…

Focused Breath

I begin with my breathing…

I'd take some loooong, slooow deeeep breaths and fill my lungs with air…

Then hold each breath for the mental count of 3…

As I sloowly exhale all the air from my mouth, I think in my mind the words deeply, deeply, deeply relaxed.

Breathe in and hold for 1-2-3.

Breathe out...Deeply, deeply, deeply relaxed.

Breathe in and hold for 1-2-3.

Breathe out...Deeply, deeply, deeply relaxed.

Breathe in and hold for 1-2-3.

Breathe out...Deeply, deeply, deeply relaxed.

Now as I breathe in, I imagine that I'm breathing in calmness and relaxation.

When I breathe out, I breathe away any tensions, anxieties, or any worries that I may be experiencing.

I feel my physical body relaxing...I feel my mind relaxing

I begin by relaxing the eyes...All the tiny muscles around the eyes...I let them relax...I just let go.

If my eyes are not already closed I might like to gently close them now,

I notice that comfortable feeling around the lids.

Perhaps even a slight fluttering there, as it takes no effort at all to allow them to close…

I know that for the next few minutes or so, there is absolutely nothing for me to do but relaax…

It's a wonderful feeling to know that there's nothing of any importance for me to do at this time but relax…

Nobody wants anything, nobody needs anything

There's no place to go right now…Theirs is nothing to do but relaax, and let go…Relaax, relax and let go.

I enjoy the wonderful feeling that is growing and developing within me now.

Relaax, let go, let go.

I know that if, at any time during this experience, any situation should arise that needs my attention, I can immediately return to full awakening consciousness, merely by counting the numbers one to five. And at the count of five I will be wide-awake, alert and fully refreshed, and able to deal effectively with any situation.

But for now, I'm just aware of the position of my body resting here.

I notice the feel of any clothing or anything else touching my body.

I take notice of the time of day. Morning, afternoon, evening, or night time…

I notice the time of the year; the temperature of the air on the skin of my hands and any other uncovered areas of my body.

I take notice of the surface beneath me and just let myself think how my awareness doesn't end there but goes all the way down, deep down, into the very center of the earth.

Relaax.

I know and trust that the universe seeks to bring me great success. I allow good things to happen to me. I know that I am able to go to a wonderful place, deep within myself and be relaxed, rejuvenated, and refreshed.

I move into a very special place, where those important changes to my life take place.

A Lazy Time

I become more and more at ease, it doesn't matter if, at times, I find my mind just wandering away to some pleasant thought, because my inner mind continues to listen and enjoys the growing sense of peace, harmony and tranquility that is growing and developing within me now.

It's those wonderful feelings that I have when sleeping soundly.

How I sometimes wish that I could just be left to doze and slumber.

I remember how I felt…lazily laying on a lawn, or on a beach in the sun…perhaps, drifting in and out of a dozing sleep.
Yaaawning and just wanting to stay where I was.

In a moment I will count slowly back from ten to zero and as I do, I will find that I relax more and more with each number of the count, until just as I've felt on those lazy occasions in the past, I feel just as deeply relaxed once again.

10…I feel myself going down…
9…lazily drifting…
8…relaxing more and more…
7…going deeper down…
6…deeper and deeper
5…halfway to total relaxation

4…I feel that wonderful, comfortable feeling…

3…2…almost there now

1…and…0…I feel totally relaaxed now

Peaceful Pool

I imagine now that I'm standing outside - in the moonlight at the top of a lovely stairway

It's a lovely warm summer's night.

The stairway is made of white marble and is lit all the way down with lamplights. I can see the stairs are wide and they wind gently down, and at the bottom of the stairs is a lovely pool.

As I look down the stairs I notice there are twenty steps leading gently down.

These are the stairs that will take me deep into relaxation.

Deep into my subconscious mind.

I begin to walk down the stairs, counting from 20 down to 0.

With each step down I relax more and more

20, 19, 18, 17, 16

I'm going deeper, deeper, and deeper.

15, 14, 13, 12, 11

I feel sooo relaxed

10, 9, 8, 7, 6

I moving into that deep relaxed state within yourself

5, 4, 3, 2, 1

I'm very relax and comfortable.

0

I'm now standing at the bottom of the stairs next to the most beautiful pool that I have ever seen.

Floating on top of the water are thousands of rose petals.

The fragrance from the roses is very noticeable and I bend down to lift a petal, noticing the velvety softness on my fingertips.

The water is very warm and inviting and so I lower myself into the water and float along on a bed of rose petals.

I imagine my body floating on the bed of rose petals, across this beautiful pool.

The water supports my body…I feel my body, bobbing gently up and down, up and down.

I imagine it…and I experience it now.

I continue floating along, really enjoying this wonderful feeling. (Pause). I let myself drift and float, drift and float, relaxing more and more with each breath that I take

For with each breath that I take and with each word that is uttered…this wonderful floating feeling fills me with a mixture of calm and tranquility

I find myself drifting and floating, to a wonderful, safe, relaxing place.

As I are floating here, safe and relaxed, it doesn't matter if, from time to time, I find my mind beginning to wander to other thoughts and feelings, because nobody wants anything, nobody needs anything…there is absolutely nothing of any importance for me to do, but relax, and let go.

I feel the warmth of the air on my body…calming my body…relaxing my body…making it feel even more tranquil, more peaceful, and even more comfortable than I can ever remember feeling.

This wonderful calm, relaxing feeling…as I float along…on this wonderful pool of peace.

From now on, whenever I want to feel as calm and relaxed and as peaceful as I feel right now, all I need to do is to close my eyes for one moment and think the word peace...

I will immediately experience the peace that I fill at this moment...peace

Place of Relaxation

I imagine now entering a lovely large elevator. The doors open and I step inside.

It's large, roomy, and very comfortable...

On one wall is a panel with buttons marking each floored from ten to B.

B represents the Basement floor, and the numbers above it represent the subsequent floors.

Once inside the lift the doors close and I press a button. As I reach each floor the button will light up and I will feel myself moving into a deeper state of relaxation.

The elevator begins to descend, and feel myself beginning to go down. As I go down I move into a deeper state of relaxation

The 9th button lights up, but the doors do not open. They remain closed and I continue to go deeper, deeper down into a profound state of relaxation

Down to the 8th floor...as you reach the 8th floor, again the doors remain closed...

I'm feeling very comfortable and very very relaxed here, and the lift goes further down to floor 7. (Pause)

Deeper deeper down now to 6. *(Pause)*

Even deeper...now. As I reach the 5th floor I become aware of how comfortable and relaxed I am at this moment.

The elevator now moves down to the 4th floor, and again, the button lights up.

Further down now to 3rd floor...I'm beginning to feel like I'm going really deep inside myself.

I reach the 2nd floor...I'm moving into an even deeper place inside of myself

Now the 1st floor...

As I reach this 1st floor the doors open, but I remain inside, because I can now see that B represents an even deeper level of relaxation. This deeper level of relaxation is found in the basement. It is known as 'the basement of relaxation'.

The lift begins to sink deep, deep, deep down and I'm relaxing more and more.

I go down past the 1st floor and now deeper down to the basement of relaxation.

The lift touches down and comes to a gentle halt…the doors open and you step outside.
It is quiet and serene here. This is a place of peace and comfort. I find that I can be Deeply, Deeply, deeply relaxed here.
I'm in a perfect state of relaxation

Private Beach

I imagine that I am out for a quiet relaxing walk…I come to a pretty winding pathway, which leads me down to the beach…I wander along relaxing deeper and deeper with every step…I so on reach the beautiful beach with miles of golden sand…I slip off my shoes and stroll across the soft sand…I gaze out into the distance…

I see the vastness of the sea ...I watch how the waves roll towards the beach...In a never-ending sequence...One after another...I hear the sound of the waves building up...Then petering out as they near the beach...

I feel a growing feeling of peace and calm...As the warm sea air lightly brushes my skin...My feet sink into the sand with every step, I take...I am relaxing deeper and deeper with every step...

I soon reach the wet sand near where the sea begins...And I notice how much louder the sea is up close...As wave after wave rolls towards me...

My feet now sink down deeper than before...Into the wet sand...When I reach the sea...I gently let my toes test the water...Which is slightly cold at first...

But soon it warms as I take a few more steps into the water...I allow the waves to roll over my feet and ankles...then they retreat again...I breathe in the fresh salty sea air...And relax deeper and deeper...

After a while, I stroll back up the beach...To a most inviting deck chair which is there especially for me...There is also a sunshade and a table...With my favorite refreshing, drink...I adjust the sunshade so that it is just right for me...I lie back in the chair with my drink...And as I take a deep breath once more...I relax deeper and deeper still as I breathe out...

I gaze out at the calm blue sea...I see the waves lapping lazily on the beach...And I hear the sound of the seagulls up above...I notice a fishing boat...With its colorful sail...Gently bobbing up and down...The sun is shining brightly...The sky is clear blue...There's not a cloud in the sky...And I am feeling more and more relaxed...

I doze in my deckchair...At this moment in time...I don't have a care in the world...

I take a deep breath once again...And as I breathe out, I relax deeper and deeper...Deep deep sleep... Deep deep sleep... Deeper and deeper than ever before...

Private Night Garden

I imagine now that I'm standing on a balcony overlooking a beautiful garden. It's a lovely warm, summer's evening, and the air is filled with the fragrant smell of sweet scented stocks and other beautiful flowers. Part of the garden is hidden and I really want to go down there.

Ten steps lead down from the balcony into the garden and I begin to walk down the steps, counting in my mind as I go down 10 – 9 – 8 – 7 – 6 - 5 - 4 – 3 – 2 – 1.

Now I'm standing at the bottom of the steps, and I can see a little grey, stony path which winds through a wooden archway into the private garden. Flower bearing Lavender clings to the archway and there are weeping willows on either side. Birds are singing tunefully in the trees and there's a soft gentle breeze – I can feel it on my skin and in my face.

Walking through into the garden I breathe in the scented night air and feel the calmness it brings to me. It's peaceful here, and it makes me feel calm - it makes me feel relaxed and I take into myself, that calm, relaxing feeling. I experience this now; that lovely, calm, relaxing feeling. It makes me feel good, makes me feel relaxed.

I'm becoming that calmer, more relaxed, more confident person. I can relax like this any time I wish. All I need to do is close my eyes for a moment and think the word calm. The word calm. And immediately I will feel just as calm, just as relaxed, as I do in my private garden.

I now imagine the word CALM – I picture it written up there in my mind, on the screen of my mind, just inside my forehead – the word CALM. I hear the word being said in my mind – it might be my voice – or some other voice that I may or may not recognize. I feel the word CALM in the centre of my being. This calmness is generated to every level of my being; every cell in my body receives the CALM and peaceful feeling.

Relaxed Loose & Comfortable

In a moment I will count slowly backwards in my mind. I will count backwards from 10 to 1. After each number I will think in my mind, the words, deeply deeply relaxed, loose, and comfortable. As I think those words in my mind, I will find that my mind and body do in fact continue to become, deeply deeply relaxed, loose, and comfortable.

Whilst I'm counting backwards with the conscious thinking mind, I'm going to be talking to the deepest part of myself, and I don't even need to consciously listen because my subconscious mind hears everything that needs to be heard.

I will allow all of the suggestions to enter into the very deepest part of my mind, that wonderful place where those important changes in my life are taking place. The words will become my thoughts and my thoughts will generate a wonderful new way of being and feeling and thinking.

I'll keep my mind focused on those numbers, counting sloowly backwards from 10 to 1 and becoming deeply deeply relaxed, loose, and comfortable. Each number that I count will make me 10 times more relaxed, loose, and comfortable.

10, deeply deeply relaxed, loose, and comfortable…

I let the forehead feel smooth and soft, the cheeks feel flat and smooth…And I just relaax…

9, deeply deeply relaxed, loose, and comfortable…

I let that relaxation spread over my entire face and let all the facial muscles relax, the tiny muscles around the mouth, the nose and the eyes.

8, deeply deeply relaxed, loose, and comfortable…

I notice the warmth there in the palms of the hands. There may also be a tingling sensation there, a tingling sensation there in the palms of the hands.

7, deeply deeply relaxed, loose, and comfortable…

Then it moves the relaxation back to the shoulders and let it flow all the way down the arms, into the wrists, the hands, the fingers, and thumbs.

6, deeply deeply relaxed, loose, and comfortable…

That relaxing feeling moves over my shoulders and into the back and relaxes the two big muscles there, one on each side of the spine.

With every count, I become 10 times more Relaxed…
With every count, I become 10 times looser…
With every count, I become 10 times more comfortable…

5, deeply deeply relaxed, loose, and comfortable…

I relax the chest and the shoulders—especially the shoulders, I just let them feel limp, loose, and comfortable…

4, deeply deeply relaxed, loose, and comfortable…

I feel the relaxing feeling flowing into the stomach, relaxing the tummy and all the muscles there.

3, deeply deeply relaxed, loose, and comfortable…

That relaxing feeling now flows down into the hips and the thighs, into the pelvic area, relaxing the pelvis and all the pelvic muscles.

2, deeply deeply relaxed, loose, and comfortable…

That relaxing sensation moves to the upper legs, & down to the knees until both the left and the right legs become deeply, deeply, deeply relaxed.

1, deeply deeply relaxed, loose, and comfortable…

I let that feeling spread all the way down my lower legs, into both calves and my ankles and then my heels.

I move my awareness, down to my feet and imagine a sensation of warmth and heaviness flowing in through feet and into the toes…

I am in a state of total relaxation…I am deeply deeply relaxed…

I am deeply deeply loose …

I am deeply deeply, and comfortable…

Secret Garden

I imagine I am in a beautiful garden…With lush manicured lawns…

There are many beautiful exotic plants all around me…The sun is shining and there is a cool caressing breeze blowing…The temperature is just as I would like it…And there is absolutely no pollen in this garden…The air here is pure and fresh…As I marvel at the vivid colors all around me…I hear the relaxing sound of birds singing overhead…

I take a deep breath…As I breathe out, I relax deeper and deeper…Deeper and deeper…

I stroll around this secret garden…Feeling the soft grass underfoot…The wonderful melody of the songbirds fill the air. The colorful flowers now appear to move in tune with every note the songbirds make…I wander towards some of the beautiful flowers...As I approach them...The scent grows more fragrant than anything I have ever experienced...The rich colors brighter than I ever seen before...I take a deep breath again...I inhale the soft warm and perfumed air...

As I breathe out...I Relax deeper and deeper...
I am more relaxed than I have ever been before. This is my secret garden grown especially for me...I come here at anytime and find that it is so easy for me to relax here...No one knows about this special place and there's no other place like my secret garden...The sun bathes me with it warm relaxing rays...The fragrance of the flowers here are sweeter than any place else...The colors are more vibrant here than any place I have ever seen...The flowers here tend to dance to every note that the songbirds sing in my secret garden....Everything is my secret garden beckons me to come, stay a while and relax.

I take a deep breath again...I inhale the sweet scented warm air of my secret garden...
And as I breathe out...I Relax deeper, deeper, and deeper...

Summer's Night

I imagine now that I'm standing outside – the sun is sitting low on the horizon.

It's a lovely clear summer's night and perfect for a garden stroll.

As I look down the stairs I notice there are twenty steps leading gently down.

There is a stone pathway of about 20 oversized stones leading into a beautifully scented garden. As I walk along the path counting the stones that makeup the walkway I notice that I am moving into a deep state of relaxation.

20, 19, 18, 17, 16
This gentle relaxing feeling reaches deep into my subconscious mind. I feel sooo relaxed

15, 14, 13, 12, 11
I continue walking along the path counting the stones and becoming more and more relaxed with every step

10, 9, 8, 7, 6
I am moving into that deeper more relaxed state. With each step I relax more and more.

5, 4, 3, 2, 1
I'm very relaxed…Relaxed and comfortable.

I'm now standing in the most beautiful and inviting gardens that I have ever seen.

I can see the sky is becoming even darker now...I allow myself to relax and be at peace here.

The garden is filled with many beautiful flowers dance in the moon's light.

The air is also filled with the delicate perfume of the roses, night scented stock, geraniums ...and other flowers. Their perfumed fragrance reaches my nostrils, making me feel even more comfortable, even more calm, even more relaxed.

In the dark, velvety sky is a full, round moon...it is surrounded by twinkling, silvery stars.

Everything here is so peaceful, everything here is so relaxing, and everything here is so calming...

I take into myself this calm...this relaxing...a peaceful feeling...

I experience it now...this calm, peaceful, relaxing feeling. I can see how good it makes me feel.

As I continue to gaze up into the velvet sky, on this calm and peaceful night, I think of the word – peace and just allow myself to think and feel the full meaning of the word peace.

From now on, whenever I want to separate from the world around me, feel free from anxiety, or whenever I want to feel as calm and relaxed and as peaceful as I feel right now, all I need to do is to close my eyes for one moment and think the word peace…

I think of my peaceful star, up there in the beautiful night sky, looking down on my body and me is engulfed in a calming peace….all the worries and anxieties that I may have been experiencing, will seem so insignificant…

They will just fade away, as once again I fill my entire body with peaceful feelings.

Whenever I want to feel as calm as I feel right now, all I need to do is close my eyes for a moment and think the word peace and allow the peace and calm to surround me and to fill me…

Peace…peace…peace

It's only a little word, but it has such beneficial effects…
Peace…And I will find, that I will immediately feel, so much calmer, so much more tranquil, so much more peaceful…just like I do at this moment in time…Peaceful…calm…relaxed

Swimming in Paradise

I can imagine that I'm now swimming in a vast ocean. I feel my body supported in the water, the waves beneath me splashing gently as I move my arms—my arms are moving—making the movements I make for swimming—I imagine this now as my arms push through the water, my head just above and my legs are moving as well, swimming, moving almost effortlessly through the water. (Pause for 10 seconds).

In front of me, all I can see is the sea, the vast ocean ahead of me, the sea goes on for miles and miles and miles, it's all around me, the sea is everywhere—and I'm so small in this enormous deep blue body of water. Occasionally, here and there is a larger splash as a fish dives out of the water and back in again, sending ripples alongside me. The sea is a lovely shade of blue and goes on, and on, and on. (Pause for 10 seconds).

My legs and my arms are moving in the movement of swimming as I move through the water, easily, effortlessly, swimming along, going nowhere in particular, reaching no place in particular, just moving through the ocean, enjoying the peacefulness and serenity of this wonderful place. (Pause for 10 seconds).

Now I can see the horizon—ahead of me—and over the horizon the sun is beginning to set. It's a glorious red and orange sunset. I see the beautiful colors—shades of red, changing from scarlet to a golden glow of orange and spreading across the sea towards me, sensational ripples of color mingling with the pacific blue sea which is becoming darker in shade—and as it becomes darker in shade I find that I can drift a little deeper into those calm and tranquil feelings that are spreading throughout my body—and whilst I'm enjoying swimming here in this beautiful place of mine, I think how nice it would be to rest and completely let go—just completely and totally relax and let go.

The sun is going down now, over the sea, gradually diminishing, becoming a little smaller as the reds and oranges magically change to warmer shades of purple and violet and crimson and the darkening sky is streaked with yellow in a breathtakingly beautiful way.

I enjoy this wonderful view. I relax a little deeper. I just relax a little deeper now and let go. For as the sun finally sets I find myself drifting down to the bottom of the sea. I'm still breathing, deeply and evenly. Listen to that breathing. Slowly and rhythmically, breathing and the sound of the waves in the ocean become one as I nestle on the seabed amongst corals and reefs and beautiful plant life and shoals of brightly colored fish that just swim right on by.

I concentrate on my breathing and I'm aware in that moment that I'm counting down from ten to zero. With each number that I count, I find that I can drift a little deeper into calmness and comfort. Safe and warm and comfortable, here in my own paradise.

The Steps

I imagine myself now, standing at the top of a long flight of steps. These steps lead down into a room, a very special room. In a moment I can walk down these steps, and as I do so I will count the steps one by one and as I walk down the steps, I will just feel myself going deeper and deeper down.

I now begin walking down as I count the steps.
10 deeper...
9 deeper...
8 deeper...
7 deeper...
6 deeper...
5 deeper...
4 deeper...
3 deeper...
2 deeper...
1 deeper...

I'm now standing at the bottom of the steps and feeling very comfortable and veery relaaxed.

Before me at the bottom of the steps is a large elegant door...I open the door and enter...I find myself now in a beautiful room.

The room is softly lit with twenty fragrant candles and there is a distant sound of lovely music.

Apart from the candle light the room is quite dark...

I can notice some beautiful, calming, peace filled colors gently moving around the room from the dancing flickering flame of the candles.

Shades of green...purple...blue...pink...violet...all the beautiful colors of the rainbow

The colors are gently moving here and there...This is a place where I can find answers or make my wildest dreams come true.

I began to count each of the candles around the room...
20...19...18...17
Each is a different height, color, and style
16...15...14...13
They also appear to invite me to stay in the room.
12...11...10...9
I feel safe here
8...7...6...5
Safe, protected and comfortable.
4...3...2...1
I allow myself to let go...and just relaax...relax...relax

Tropical Garden

I imagine that I'm standing at the entrance of a very deep cave. Looking down I can see the entrance of the cave and it feels warm, inviting, and safe.

Many steps lead deep down into the cave and I begin to walk down the steps, counting in my mind as I go down.

15 – 14 – 13 – 12 – 11– I arrive at a small landing and walk across the landing to the next flight of steps. I notice that as I move down the stairs, I'm wrapped in a peaceful, calm, and inviting energy.

I continue down the next flight of stairs 10 - 9 – 8 – 7 - 6…I come to the next landing. This is a quiet peaceful place. There's a cool breeze blowing and I can see colorful lights dancing around the walls and a beautiful glowing light coming from the cave below. I walk over to the final flight of steps, counting again as I continue down 5 – 4 – 3 – 2 – 1. There's a warm inviting sensation here that beckons all who enter to come and enjoy.

I'm standing at the bottom of the steps.

Looking deeper into the glowing part of the cave I see a narrowing where the way is lit with torches. I walk towards the light until I see more steps, leading deeper into the cave. Treading carefully now, little pools of water are scattered on the floor of the cave – I go carefully down – deeper down – to a deeper part of the cave – the lights grow brighter as the cave widens and I come across a beautiful tropical garden.

A small path leads through the garden. On either side of the path are many large and beautiful plants and small animals – huge ferns with multi colored foliage – there are deer and rabbits and squirrels and a doe stops in her tracks and, standing on her hind legs, turns to look at me. The air is still, warm, and humid and on the trees are butterflies, bigger and more brightly colored than I ever dreamt possible. I feel at one with the plant and the animal kingdom and I feel the energy from the plants and the animals.

I feel at one with all of creation

Tropical Island

I imagine that I'm strolling along on a beautiful, tropical island. It's a warm, sunny afternoon; the sky is a lovely shade of blue and the sea a startling shade of blue-green. The waves are dancing and splashing up to the shore and the soft white sand is warm underneath my bare feet.

As I slowly walk along on the soft white sand, I can feel the soft grains of sand between my toes, and I'm taking in the beautiful view, the blue-green sea, the lovely white sand, and the clear blue sky. Further along the beach silhouetted against the blue sky are palm trees. I notice the deck chairs shaded with straw umbrellas. But there's no one else in sight, there's just the sound of birds singing some place in the distance. It's so calm here, and so peaceful.

This is my paradise. My own, very special, very private place, where I can come, and relax, at anytime I wish. I always remember that. I can come here any time that I want to – all with the power of my own mind – all I need to do is relax – relax – relax – and relax.

I wonder if I can now I imagine myself sitting down here – finding a comfortable place to sit, on the sand. As I find a comfortable place to sit, I can see the sea, and the sparkling sunlight is reflecting ripples on the surface of the sea – and everything is so calm – and so peaceful – and I take into myself that calm and peaceful feeling – so calm, so peaceful – and so tranquil.

I'm just sitting here, on the soft, white sand and I can smell the fresh salt sea air – I can even taste the fresh, salt sea air. I can taste it in my lungs and on my lips – I experience it all now, that lovely fresh sea air, feel, and experience that sea air. And I breathe in pure air. I breathe in pure air, deep into my lungs – I experience it now – I feel and experience that lovely fresh sea air. I feel the freshness and strength that it brings to me. I breathe in that lovely, fresh sea air and just see how good it makes me feel.

I'm sitting here; just sitting here; listening to the sound of the waves dancing and splashing against the shore and the sound of the sea birds in the distance and I begin to feel a gentle breeze against my skin. The sun, so warm, against my body, I can feel the light from the sun radiating around my body, warming me gently, all over my body.

I can feel the warmth from the sun now and I imagine that I can direct the sunlight over my body, starting with both of my feet at the same time and then up my legs, my calves, my thighs, my hips, my pelvic area and my stomach and chest. I move the heat up and down my body, down and up, up and down, and then let it flow over my shoulders and into my back, and all the way down the back of my body, and up again back to my shoulders and down my arms to the tips of my fingers.

I move the heat up and down my arms, down and up, up and down, and then let it flow on up into my neck, my throat and into my face, relaxing all of my facial muscles, and on up over my eyes and forehead into the crown of my head.

Now I imagine the light from the heat of the sun entering the crown of my head and like a tornado soaring down the inside of my body, down and down and down and down.

Going deeper and deeper down. Deeper and deeper and deeper down. The further down I go, the more relaxed and the more comfortable I become, until my entire body, from the top of my head all the way down to the tips of my toes are completely and totally relaxed.

And now I'm going to count down from ten to one and each number will take me deeper and deeper into complete relaxation. 10 – 9 – 8 – 7 – 6 - 5 – 4 – 3 – 2 – 1.

I know that I can return to this wonderful peaceful tropical island at anytime. It will always invite me and receive me with loving energies. It will always await my return.

Winding Staircase

I'm now standing at the top of a very long and beautiful winding staircase. There are a hundred steps leading down, and around and although I can't see the bottom of the stairs from here, I just know that there's a beautiful place waiting at the bottom of the stairs, just for me.

I notice the staircase; I notice the carpet if there is one, It's my favorite color.

Perhaps the stairs are made of marble or wood, either type is okay.

On either side is a beautiful firm banister that makes me feel safe and secure. The banister is smooth and polished, and I place my hand lightly on it.

I notice that on the floor of the stairs are the numbers from one hundred, going all the way down to zero.

The further down I go, the more comfortable and the more relaxed I become.
I now begin walking down the stairs. I'm stepping down, down, down.

With every step that I take I go deeper…deeper and deeper down.

Relaxing more and more with each step down.

I look down at the numbers and take notice of what number step I'm on.

I'm about halfway down the staircase now. I continue going down the staircase… deeper, deeper, relaxing more and more.

I've reach the bottom step. As I step down, the staircase fades away.

I'm deeply relaxed now, very deeply relaxed…

From the top of my head, aaaall the way down…deeper down, to the tips of my toes I am relaxed, relaxed, relaxed…

Section 4
Color Scripts B

Aquamarine

Each and every time I see the color aquamarine consciously or unconsciously my desire and determination to succeed in EVERY area of my life will continue growing stronger, stronger, and stronger. Each and every suggestion I have received here in this session will continue to work more and more effectively every time I see the color AQUAMARINE…AQUAMARINE…AQUAMARINE.

Black

Each and every time I see the color black consciously or subconsciously my desire and determination to succeed in EVERY area of my life will continue growing stronger, stronger, and stronger. Each and every suggestion I have received here in this session will continue to work more and more effectively every time I see the color BLACK…BLACK…BLACK.

Blue

Each and every time I see the color blue consciously or subconsciously my desire and determination to succeed in EVERY area of my life will continue growing stronger, stronger, and stronger. Each and every suggestion I have received here in this session will continue to work more and more effectively every time I see the color BLUE…BLUE…BLUE. Each and every suggestion I have received here in this session will continue to work more and more effectively every time I see the color BLUE…BLUE…BLUE.

Brown

Each and every time I see the color brown consciously or unconsciously my desire and determination to succeed in EVERY area of my life will continue growing stronger, stronger, and stronger. Each and every suggestion I have received here in this session will continue to work more and more effectively every time I see the color BROWN…BROWN…BROWN.

Fuchsia

Each and every time I see the color fuchsia consciously or subconsciously my desire and determination to succeed in EVERY area of my life will continue growing stronger, stronger, and stronger. Each and every suggestion I have received here in this session will continue to work more and more effectively every time I see the color FUSHIA…FUSHIA…FUSHIA.

Gold

Each and every time I see the color gold consciously or subconsciously my desire and determination to succeed in EVERY area of my life will continue growing stronger, stronger, and stronger. Each and every suggestion I have received here in this session will continue to work more and more effectively every time I see the color GOLD...GOLD...GOLD.

Green

Each and every time I see the color green consciously or subconsciously my desire and determination to succeed in EVERY area of my life will continue growing stronger, stronger, and stronger. Each and every suggestion I have received here in this session will continue to work more and more effectively every time I see the color GREEN...GREEN...GREEN.

Grey

Each and every time I see the color grey consciously or subconsciously my desire and determination to succeed in EVERY area of my life will continue growing stronger, stronger, and stronger. Each and every suggestion I have received here in this session will continue to work more and more effectively every time I see the color GREY...GREY...GREY.

Orange

Each and every time I see the color orange consciously or subconsciously my desire and determination to succeed in EVERY area of my life will continue growing stronger, stronger, and stronger. Each and every suggestion I have received here in this session will continue to work more and more effectively every time I see the color ORANGE…ORANGE…ORANGE.

Pink

Each and every time I see the color pink consciously or subconsciously my desire and determination to succeed in EVERY area of my life will continue growing stronger, stronger, and stronger. Each and every suggestion I have received here in this session will continue to work more and more effectively every time I see the color PINK…PINK…PINK.

Purple

Each and every time I see the color purple consciously or subconsciously my desire and determination to succeed in EVERY area of my life will continue growing stronger, stronger, and stronger. Each and every suggestion I have received here in this session will continue to work more and more effectively every time I see the color PURPLE…PURPLE…PURPLE.

Red

Each and every time I see the color red consciously or subconsciously my desire and determination to succeed in EVERY area of my life will continue growing stronger, stronger, and stronger. Each and every suggestion I have received here in this session will continue to work more and more effectively every time I see the color RED…RED…RED.

Silver

Each and every time I see the color silver consciously or subconsciously my desire and determination to succeed in EVERY area of my life will continue growing stronger, stronger, and stronger. Each and every suggestion I have received here in this session will continue to work more and more effectively every time I see the color SILVER...SILVER...SILVER.

Turquoise

Each and every time I see the color turquoise consciously or subconsciously my desire and determination to succeed in EVERY area of my life will continue growing stronger, stronger, and stronger. Each and every suggestion I have received here in this session will continue to work more and more effectively every time I see the color TURQUOISE...TURQUOISE...TURQUOISE.

Violet

Each and every time I see the color violet consciously or subconsciously my desire and determination to succeed in EVERY area of my life will continue growing stronger, stronger, and stronger. Each and every suggestion I have received here in this session will continue to work more and more effectively every time I see the color VIOLET...VIOLET...VIOLET.

White

Each and every time I see the color white consciously or subconsciously my desire and determination to succeed in EVERY area of my life will continue growing stronger, stronger, and stronger. Each and every suggestion I have received here in this session will continue to work more and more effectively every time I see the color WHITE…WHITE…WHITE.

Yellow

Each and every time I see the color YELLOW consciously or subconsciously my desire and determination to succeed in EVERY area of my life will continue growing stronger, stronger, and stronger. Each and every suggestion I have received here in this session will continue to work more and more effectively every time I see the color YELLOW…YELLOW…YELLOW.

Section 5
Suggestions

BUSINESS

Business 1

1. I develop good and prosperous business partnerships
2. I always see the small details and the big picture in all situations
3. Business answers come to me in my waking state and in my dream state
4. Business information and answers come to me quickly
5. I run my business effectively and efficiently
6. Clients flock to my organization
7. My business provides me with a prosperous lifestyle
8. My have very low overhead
9. My bottom-line is always in the green
10. I have very excellent business connections
11. All of my employees are happy, well trained, and productive

Business 2

1. Everyday is a successful day of business
2. I am very decisive concerning business matters
3. I make very effective business decisions

4. I am calm and relaxed throughout the business day
5. My thinking is sharp and precise
6. My mind is focused on profitable business matters
7. I always accomplish the daily goals that I set
8. I always make excellent use of my time
9. I am open to new profitable ideas
10. I improve my business daily
11. I manage and use my resources wisely

Business 3

1. All situations happen to benefit my business
2. I am a very happy and very successful business owner
3. I make wise business investments
4. My business advertising dollars are used well
5. My business has excellent customer service
6. The value of my business increases daily
7. I have sound business practices
8. I have a top-notch business
9. My business has a very large profit margin
10. My business has a very large amount of customer traffic
11. I have a very sound and lucrative business

Product Oriented 1

1. I provide products that people want and need
2. My products are always in high demand
3. I get great deals on the products that I carry
4. My customers make my products fly off the shelves

5. My employee s are efficient at selling all company products
6. My customers feel my products are priced economically and very reasonable
7. My customers are quick to settle their account balances
8. All customer sales orders are paid full when my business issues them
9. I get enormous amounts of products at extremely low cost to me
10. All of my products sell out fast

Product Oriented 2
1. My business has a very large amount of customer traffic
2. My business has an enormously large steady flow of paying customer
3. I have a large customer base of high volume buyers
4. I have a large volume of satisfied customers
5. My products are innovative and cutting edge
6. I always get fresh ideas for new products to offer my customers
7. I am always researching new products that will bring increase to my business
8. Word of mouth brings large volumes of customers to my business daily
9. My business has a very large amount of customer traffic
10. My business provides me with a very prosperous lifestyle

Service Oriented 1
1. I provide services that people want and need
2. My services are always in high demand

3. My services I provide are cost efficient for me
4. My clients quickly order my services
5. My clients feel my prices are economical and very reasonable
6. My clients are quick to settle their account balances
7. All client invoices are paid in full within days after my business issues them
8. All of the services my business provide are extremely low cost to me
9. My clients quickly pay the asking price for my business services
10. My business has an enormously large steady flow of paying clients

Service Oriented 2

1. I have a large client base of high volume buyers
2. I have a large volume of satisfied clients
3. My employees are efficient at selling all company services
4. My services are innovative and cutting edge
5. I always get fresh ideas for new services to offer my clients
6. I am always researching new products that will bring increase to my business
7. I always get fresh new ideas and ways to increase the services that we provide
8. Word of mouth brings large volumes of clients to my business daily
9. My business has a very large amount of client traffic
10. My business provides me with a prosperous lifestyle

Business Success 1

1. I work towards the success of my business everyday
2. I accept success in my business ventures
3. I enjoy great success in my business
4. I believe in myself and the success of my business
5. I accomplish all of my jobs
6. I treat customers and clients with respect
7. I consider all comments and questions submitted
8. I balance the budget of my business effectively
9. I handle new customers easily and with satisfaction
10. My business grows and expands exponentially

Business Success 2

1. My business impresses people
2. My business receives large amounts of money for its services or products
3. I use old and new ideas to improve my business
4. I learn something every time I work
5. I welcome new business opportunities
6. I invest wisely in my business
7. I am very business savvy
8. I am professional in all business matters
9. I increase my value every day
10. I go the extra mile for my business

Business Success 3

1. I establish long-lasting business relationships
2. My work makes people happy
3. My work benefits people, communities, and society
4. I make my business worthwhile
5. I plan for the future of my business
6. I am happy when I succeed
7. I manage the money of my business effectively
8. I use business resources wisely
9. I make wise choices concerning business advertisements
10. I welcome new constructive business ideas

Business Success 4

1. I am decisive in all business matters
2. I make important business decisions easily and quickly
3. I think sharply and accurately in business situations
4. I am calm and quick witted in business dealings
5. I am relaxed and focused at all times
6. I am focused and calm when handling business matters
7. I am responsible in business matters
8. My business success allows me to help others
9. Money comes to my business quickly and easily
10. My business is a money magnet

Selling Power 1

1. I believe in myself and my abilities
2. I believe in my products

3. My sales benefit me and serves others
4. I always make successful sells
5. I sell with ease
6. I am a very strong closer
7. Sells have made me very prosperous
8. I am an innovative salesperson
9. I am persistent
10. I am persuasive and successful

Selling Power 2
1. I am an enthusiastic seller
2. I attract abundance through my sells
3. I quickly and successfully close all of my sales
4. I adapt well in all situations
5. I am successful at selling
6. I am always finding ways to improve my selling skills
7. I manage my time very well
8. I am a mega salesperson
9. I achieve all of my selling goals
10. I enjoy selling

Selling Power 3
1. I help others through sells
2. I enjoy people and helping them
3. My confidence is always high and strong
4. I generate leads
5. I get referrals easily

6. I create success in all that I do
7. I set sells goals and achieve them quickly
8. My thoughts are clear and precise
9. I am focus and determined
10. I achieve all of my sells goals

Selling Power 4

1. Selling has made me a big success
2. I receive wealth from sells
3. I am a self-starter
4. I am very efficient
5. My sales increase exponentially
6. I am energetic and happy
7. My selling always bring me prosperity
8. I have an edge when it comes to selling
9. I always rise to any occasion
10. My performance is always outstanding
11. Sales have made me very prosperous

CONFIDENCE

Confidence 1

1. I give closure to the past
2. I have unlimited possibilities
3. I move forward to fulfill my destiny

4. I welcome change in my life
5. I adjust to change in my life
6. My future is full of possibilities
7. I invite new choices into my life
8. I live free to live and experience life
9. I manifest my goals daily
10. I find what I need within me

Confidence 2

1. I welcome the future
2. Change in my life is a way for me to learn
3. The plan of my life reveals itself naturally
4. New realms of possibility are open to me
5. I accept peace and joy into my life
6. I learn valuable lessons from change
7. I am in control of my life
8. I'm ready to live life to its fullest
9. I nurture my inner child
10. I love my inner child
11. I allow my inner child to heal

Confidence 3

1. I claim my creative power now
2. I am discovering how wonderful I am
3. I see within myself a magnificent being
4. I am wise and beautiful
5. I am confident in who I am an in my abilities

6. I love what I see in me
7. I am whole and complete
8. I choose to love and enjoy myself
9. I am my own woman
10. I am in charge of my life

Confidence 4

1. I expand my capabilities
2. I am free to be all that I can be
3. I have a great life and I enjoy it
4. My life is filled with love
5. The love in my life begins with me
6. I have dominion over my life
7. I am a powerful person
8. I am worthy of love and respect
9. I am subject to no one
10. I am free to be me

Confidence 5

1. I am willing to learn new ways of living
2. I stand on my own two feet
3. I accept and use my own power
4. I am at peace with being single or married
5. I rejoice and enjoy where I am
6. I love and enjoy myself for who I am
7. I love, support, and enjoy the people in my life
8. I am deeply fulfilled by life

9. I explore all the many avenues of love
10. I love being a who I am

Confidence 6

1. I love being alive at this point in time and space
2. I fill my life with love
3. I accept my gift of alone time with myself
4. I feel totally complete and whole
5. I give myself all that I need
6. It is safe for me to grow
7. I enjoy being bold and independent
8. I am safe and secure
9. All is well in my world
10. I make myself complete and whole

Confidence 7

1. I believe in myself 100 percent
2. I always act in a way that is beneficial
3. I believe in my abilities
4. I am fully confident in myself
5. I think about the results of my actions
6. I rely upon my judgments
7. My confidence increases exponentially
8. I believe wholly in myself
9. I am very successful
10. I am tremendously confident

Confidence 8

1. I accept who I am
2. I am happy when I succeed
3. I think of positive outcomes
4. I am my own person
5. I have infinite self-esteem
6. Motivation comes freely to me
7. I believe entirely in myself
8. My future is determined by me
9. I always think positively about myself
10. I control my own self-confidence

Confidence 9

1. I work towards improving my life
2. I am in total control of my destiny
3. I seek help when needed
4. I think about myself in positive ways
5. I stand behind all of my decisions
6. I grow more confident in myself everyday
7. I am confident in my dealings and feelings
8. I am more confident each day
9. I make wise choices and I stand behind them
10. My confidence and my abilities are continually growing

Confidence 10

1. I am brilliant and capable
2. I am unlimited and goal oriented

3. I am able to accomplish all that I set out to do
4. I exude confidence
5. I am a responsible leader
6. My thoughts are powerful and bring about change
7. My mind is full of purposeful thoughts
8. I am powerful and motivated
9. I am sharp witted and productive
10. I am empowered by the energy of thought

Confidence 11

1. I am able to quickly achieve my goals
2. I am empowered by the energy of creativity
3. I take the right action and get good results
4. I am motivated and energetic
5. I act enthusiastically
6. I follow through with all of my undertakings
7. I am enthused about my goals
8. I feel great and I love life
9. I feel really good about myself
10. I exude sincerity and confidence

Confidence 12

1. I am confidence and full of life
2. I am liked by the people that are important to me
3. I believe in myself and my abilities
4. I only have thoughts that are beneficial to me
5. I only have relationships that are beneficial to me

6. I am focused and attuned to my goals
7. I trust myself and my decisions
8. I am a winner and very successful
9. I am very good at what I do
10. I like myself and I have achieved great things

Confidence 13

1. I love life and I enjoy living
2. I am loved by friends, family, and associates
3. I am secure and confident
4. I enjoy myself and life
5. I accept others for who they are
6. Life is a school and I enjoy learning
7. I accept learning because it helps me grow
8. I am whole, complete, and confident
9. I am focused and productive
10. I am very confident in myself

Confidence 14

1. I can do anything I set my mind to do
2. I am very proud of myself and my accomplishments
3. My self-esteem is very high
4. I am very valuable to society
5. I have great confidence in myself and my abilities
6. My self-worth is infinite
7. I am limitless in my abilities
8. I attain everything I desire

9. My self-esteem increases every day
10. I accept myself wholly

Confidence 15

1. I accept every aspect of myself
2. I cherish what I say
3. I cherish and enjoy what I do
4. I cherish what I believe
5. I love myself wholly
6. I am able to achieve great things
7. I believe in myself
8. I know who I am
9. I listen to my heart and inner voice
10. I know and trust my abilities

Confidence 16

1. I speak positively about myself
2. I think positive thoughts about myself
3. I listen to my dreams
4. I follow my dreams
5. I am the best
6. My healthy self-image keeps me successful
7. I enjoy what I do
8. I attain my dreams
9. I enjoy living life
10. I am happy attaining my dreams

CREATIVITY

Creativity 1
1. All that I need is within me
2. The wisdom and creativity of the Universe is within me
3. I apply the creative wisdom of the Universe to every situation
4. I am a very creative being
5. I was born to create and I do it very well
6. I handle every situation creatively
7. My abilities evolve and progress at a rapid rate
8. I have a healthy desire to grow and learn
9. My subconscious mind taps into the Universal Mind when needed
10. My latent abilities easily manifest on the physical plain
11. I quickly tap into my hidden potential

Creativity 2
1. I effortlessly fulfill my destiny through my creative abilities
2. I am able to activate my creative abilities at will
3. My creative abilities intensify with each use
4. My creativity grows daily
5. I draw my inspiration from the Universe
6. I quickly draw from my subconscious mind
7. I utilize the limitless abilities of the super-conscious mind
8. I am at one with the unlimited divine inspiration
9. Every opportunity brings me a creative advantage

10. My prosperity is tied to my creativity
11. My creativity is activated whenever it is needed

Creativity 3

1. My creative mind is always alert and working
2. I possess boundless creative abilities
3. I am an unlimited source of creativity
4. The creativity of the universe flows to and through me
5. I experience and operate in the highest levels of creativity
6. I experience the highest levels of imagination
7. I am creative in all aspects of my life
8. My creativity contributes to the lives of others
9. I am able to express myself through my creativity
10. I am always imaginative and creative
11. I see creative solutions easily and quickly

Creativity 4

1. Creativity comes easily to me
2. I receive creative inspiration from the universe
3. I am a natural creative genius
4. Creativity flows to and through me
5. I am creative and ingenious
6. My life is filled with creative thoughts
7. I have unlimited creative abilities
8. My life is filled with creative words
9. My life is filled with creative actions
10. My creativity flows to help me and others

11. I am creative and ingenious

CRITICISM

Criticism 1
1. I take criticism positively
2. I critique my own work
3. I accept criticism as a critiquing tool from others
4. I use constructive criticism to improve
5. I recognize and use beneficial acts and words
6. I receive comments with grace and charm
7. I examine criticism wisely
8. I view criticism as an opinion poll
9. Positive criticism helps me succeed
10. Second opinions are welcome

Criticism 2
1. I logically examine all criticism
2. I accept criticism over my work and myself
3. I find the point to all criticism
4. I handle remarks calmly
5. I build my character using constructive criticism
6. I improve my skills with advice
7. I listen to positive criticism
8. I think calmly at all times
9. I give positive criticism
10. I criticize others and myself positively

11. I decide who or what I listen to

DECISIONS

Decisions 1
1. I make quick decisions easily
2. I am very decisive
3. I am organized
4. I am very thorough
5. I know how and when to make decisions
6. I always make the right decisions
7. I construct a clear plan of action
8. I clearly layout all things when making a decision
9. I keep my priorities in order
10. I am well informed when making decisions

Decisions 2
1. I think through every action
2. I ask for help when I need it
3. I express my ideas clearly
4. I am able to obtain accurate information
5. I stand behind my decisions
6. I am clear and concise when making decisions
7. I am single-minded when making decisions
8. I am very matter of fact when making decisions
9. I am a very decisive person

10. Decisions are easy to make

Decisions 3
1. I make correct decisions
2. I give helpful advice
3. It is easy to decide what is right
4. I seek help when needed
5. I am calm when making decisions
6. I assess every situation before making a decision
7. I see myself as a good, helpful, and fair leader
8. I create a positive future for myself and others when making decisions
9. I analyze every possible outcome before making a decision
10. I do what benefits everyone

Decisions 4
1. I find creative solutions to problems and situations
2. I always find the best solution
3. I am a natural decision maker
4. I choose the best outcome in a timely manner
5. I create new solutions to every problem
6. I find the cause of problems easily
7. I make excellent decisions in every situation
8. I take pleasure in helping others decide
9. I am confident and believe in my decisions
10. I see main problems clearly
11. I make decisions with love

DESIRES

Desires 1

1. I clearly form my desires
2. I state my desires with precision
3. I clearly visualize obtaining all of my desires
4. I am open about what I desire
5. I use my resources to get what I desire
6. I know how to obtain my desires
7. I am motivated to get what I desire
8. The Universe works hard to bring all of my desires to me
9. The Universe fulfills my desires out of its abundance
10. I know exactly what I desire

Desires 2

1. I make time to obtain my desires
2. I research ways to get what I desire
3. My desires move me along a path to my destiny
4. I make friends with people that are key to bringing my desires to me
5. I respect and honor my desires
6. My desires come from my Higher Self/God
7. My desires are the Universe's way of blessing me
8. I am confident in my actions and desires
9. I go for what I desire
10. I honor the Universe by forming and having desires

Desires 3

1. I gracefully obtain all that I desire
2. The Universe races to fulfill all of my desires
3. I enjoy talking about my desired goals
4. I feel good getting what I desire
5. I make my desires known
6. The Universe presents many opportunities for my desires to be fulfilled
7. I take advantage of every good opportunity that is presented to me
8. My desires demonstrate what is waiting for me
9. I honor the Universe by obtaining my desires
10. I am comfortable with my desires

ENERGY

Energy 1

1. Each and everyday I feel more and more energetic
2. I feel more alive everyday
3. My energy encourages cooperation from others
4. I am always full of energy
5. The energy in my environment is always vibrant and healthy
6. I have more than enough energy to accomplish all of the day's goals
7. My environment is full of positive constructive energy

8. My energy is calm and productive
9. The energy of the universe moves through me
10. I have a healthful energy that helps me exercise regularly

Energy 2
1. My energy is always at a level for peak performance
2. I start my day fully energized
3. My energy level increases automatically when needed
4. I awaken each day energetically refreshed and alert
5. I have a boundless supply of energy
6. I have the energy of a winner
7. I am energetically able to perform all of the day's tasks and activities
8. My energy levels allow me to accomplish my goals swiftly
9. I perform my daily routines effortlessly
10. My vibrant energy brings life to everything around me

Energy 3
1. I breathe in a manner that nourishes my energy levels
2. My energy is always centered and grounded
3. My energy invokes enthusiasm in others
4. My energy grows stronger and stronger each day
5. I maintain a high level of energy through my day
6. I have a high metabolism rate
7. My energy level decreases at the end of the day when it's time to rest
8. My energy allows me to multi-task efficiently

9. My energy is vibrant
10. My energy is always full of life

EXAMS

Exam 1
1. I know my material before taking an exam
2. I do very well on exams
3. Taking exams is fun and simple for me
4. I am perfectly relaxed when taking exams
5. My mind is infinite
6. My learning capacity improves daily
7. I sleep easily as preparation for an exam
8. I complete exams on time
9. I strive to surpass my previous accomplishments
10. I am calm and motivated during exams

Exam 2
1. I recall information easily and precisely
2. I write essays with ease
3. I have excellent recall abilities
4. I exercise my mind daily
5. Taking exams is easy for me
6. I ask for help when needed
7. I use old tests to help me learn

8. I make good use of every resource
9. Studying is easy for me
10. I have precise result oriented study habits

Exam 3

1. The correct answers come with ease
2. My aptitude increases daily
3. I know the material on my exams
4. I choose the correct answers quickly
5. Test taking is a breeze for me
6. I spend quality time in study everyday
7. Studying is fun for me
8. I am wide-awake during study time and exams
9. I keep myself well rested
10. I recall lecture information easily

Exam 4

1. I use questions to find answers
2. Answers come to me easily
3. I listen to my intuition
4. Scoring high on exams is easy and natural to me
5. I see exams as a training tool
6. I write my answers legibly
7. I take breaks when needed
8. Studying is easy for me
9. I break complex things into simple ones
10. I am relaxed during exams

Exam 5

1. I take my studies seriously
2. I enjoy my study time because it helps me grow
3. I spend quality time studying
4. I am thorough in learning my study material
5. All of the info that I have received is stored in my mind and can easily be recalled at will
6. I am able to understand each exam question and answer it quickly
7. Studying and taking exams is part of my learning process and I enjoy the entire process
8. I enjoy reading and studying material
9. I enjoy preparing for exams and taking exams
10. I enjoy taking exams and tests

Exam 6

1. I have a proven method that helps me score high on exams
2. Taking an exam lets me show how much I've progressed along a path
3. Exams are very easy to take
4. My study techniques are very productive
5. Scoring high on an exam is effortless
6. I always score in the highest percentile when taking an exam
7. I get very calm and relaxed when given an opportunity to take an exam
8. I move through every exam quickly and with ease
9. I complete each test in record time
10. I draw from all levels of mind during an exam

Exam 7

1. Information flows quickly from Infinite Mind when I take exams
2. I trust the information that I receive from my subconscious mind when taking exams
3. I retain all information that is needed to score well on exams
4. I recall all the information that I need to score high on exams
5. It is very easy for me to correctly answer exam questions
6. I always remember far more than I realize
7. I'm always calm and happy when taking an exam
8. I read each question carefully then correctly and thoroughly answer each one
9. I finish every exam with high scores and flying colors
10. I always feel good about taking an exam

Exam 8

1. Exams give me the opportunity to show how much I've learned
2. I always prepare for my exams by studying
3. I fully focus on the questions during an exam
4. I can take an exam at anytime with little to no advance notice and score high on it
5. I am always fully prepared to take an exam and make a high score
6. I recall the correct answers because I'm thoroughly prepared
7. I am always relaxed when taking an exam
8. My mind is clear and sharp during an exam
9. I'm very confident about taking exams
10. I am always prepared for every exam

GOALS

Goals 1
1. I keep my life organized
2. I always set goals for myself
3. I am in control of my thoughts, actions, and life
4. I am well informed
5. I live the life I desire because I obtain my goals
6. I am always well prepared
7. I keep abreast of the latest techniques and information
8. I measure my progress by my goals
9. I stay on track to achieve my goals
10. I maintain disciple throughout my life

Goals 2
1. I reach and obtain my goals in record time
2. I adjust my actions when needed
3. I keep all of my thoughts and actions moving towards my goals
4. I only consider positive thoughts
5. I have a clear concise plan of action that will help me obtain my goals
6. Every event, situation, and circumstance helps me reach my goals
7. My pace is steady to reach my goals in record time
8. My thoughts are positive and workable
9. I am always progress towards my goals
10. I calculate all of my actions

Goals 3

1. I maintain a steady course
2. My progression towards my goals is steady
3. I am modest and humble
4. I am a headstrong negotiator
5. I know what it takes to reach my goals
6. I always make my desired goals my reality
7. The Universe has said yes to me concerning my goals
8. I am always moving forward towards my goals
9. My goals help me get the most out of life
10. My goals are always obtainable
11. The Universe assists me in reaching all of my goals

HEALTH

Health 1

1. I am always calm and relaxed
2. I am the picture of health
3. I always feel good
4. My body always feels excellent and comfortable
5. My cells remember their state of perfection
6. My cells produce a continuous healthy state in my body
7. I am focused and always healthy
8. I enjoy optimal health all the time
9. My body is perfect, whole, energetic, and healthy

10. Unlimited good health is mine Divine right

Health 2
1. My organs are always working for me in perfect order
2. My tissues are in perfect working order
3. My body adjust when needed to maintain an excellent state of health
4. My cells stay in perfect working order
5. I live in Divine health
6. My organs operate in perfect harmony
7. My tissues are working in perfect harmony
8. My cells are always working for me in perfect harmony
9. I eat healthy
10. I maintain a healthy lifestyle

Health 3
1. I get rest that rejuvenates my body in every way
2. My entire body and being is working in perfect order and perfect harmony
3. I have a health attitude and mindset
4. I have full range of motion in my entire body
5. My actions keep me healthy
6. My mind keeps me healthy
7. I engage in healthy activities
8. I accept only healthy things
9. My thoughts promote good health
10. I always see myself in a good state of health

INNER ADVISOR

Inner Advisor 1

1. I have an inner advisor
2. I am very comfortable discussing things with my inner advisor
3. I am able to obtain any answer
4. My inner voice brings information to me whenever it's needed
5. Answers and information flow from my inner advisor
6. I enjoy consulting with my inner advisor
7. I receive very helpful information from my inner advisor
8. I can ask any question
9. I consult my inner advisor with any and all concerns
10. Solutions come to me with ease from my inward source

Inner Advisor 2

1. My inner advisor is my direct connection with the universe
2. I patiently await clues
3. Answers always come to me swiftly from my inner source
4. I receive information through all of my senses
5. Symbols appear to bring me information
6. My inner advisor uses the words of any language to give me information
7. Ideas come to me from my inner advisor
8. My inner advisor will always lead me in the right direction
9. I consult my inner advisor daily
10. I can speak with my inner advisor whenever the need arises

JOB MOTIVATION

Job Motivation 1
1. I enjoy my profession
2. I am a clear thinker
3. I am decisive and enjoy making decisions
4. I am able to see all details
5. I always look at the big picture
6. I strategize in my mind
7. My profession brings prosperity to me
8. I am a positive thinker and I get positive results
9. I am result oriented
10. I do extremely well in my chosen profession

Job Motivation 2
1. I manage my time very well
2. I am a quick learner
3. I make full use of my professional contacts
4. I am always polishing and honing my skills
5. I am always prompt and prepared
6. I am part of a winning team of professionals
7. My profession allows me to be an excellent provider
8. My family has many advantages because of my profession
9. I start each day energized, alert, and confident
10. I complete all my daily tasks

Job Motivation 3
1. I work very well with others
2. I handle every situation and challenge with confidence
3. I easily excel in my profession
4. My profession allows me to help others
5. I enjoy challenges that I encounter in my profession
6. I am well organized at work
7. I remain balanced in all areas of my life
8. I treat myself well
9. My associates and coworkers enjoy working with me
10. I am always well rested

Job Motivation 4
1. I have a very helpful network of people
2. I conduct myself well in every forum
3. I am articulate and relay my thoughts and ideas well
4. I always bring positive information to discussions and meetings
5. I am able to sleep well after a day at work
6. I am calm, cool, and collected under pressure
7. I work hard then play hard
8. I am always developing my professional skills
9. Challenges at work improve me
10. I motivate others very well

Job Motivation 5
1. My profession brings lucrative rewards to me
2. I easily employ the help and cooperation of others
3. My ability to adapt and reason gives me an edge
4. I am always improving my mind
5. I continually educate myself
6. I have an excellent relationship with my associates
7. I am always finding ways to improve myself
8. I work well alone and with a team
9. I always bring fresh new ideas to my profession
10. I keep up on the latest technology and information concerning my profession

Job Motivation 6
1. I am an enterprising person
2. I am an excellent self-starter
3. I am very motivated
4. I enjoy acquiring new skills
5. My profession brings me the recognition that I deserve
6. I uses creativity in all that I do
7. My profession is very rewarding to me
8. I make very good advances in my profession
9. I speak and present myself very well in my profession
10. Working in my profession brings prosperity to me

MOTIVATION

Motivation 1
1. Greatness is my portion
2. I continuously challenge myself
3. I have been empowered to succeed
4. I possess great confidence
5. I have an excellent reputation
6. I see the big picture and the smallest details
7. I am bold
8. I accomplish all of my undertakings
9. I am always increasing my knowledge
10. I am an honorable person

Motivation 2
1. I am visited by very influential people
2. I gain strength from the smallest of things
3. I am an expert in my field
4. The Glory of the Almighty is my crown
5. I have mastered my craft
6. I am mindful of all things that were created
7. I only have positive thoughts
8. I am a leader
9. I am highly skilled in many areas
10. I am an excellent representative

Motivation 3

    11. I have a secret place of refuge

    12. I am able to retreat into a fortress when needed

    13. I have a life of peace and safety

    14. I use truth as my shield

    15. The Angels assisting me at all times

    16. Truth provides great protection for me

    17. Good things are always happening for me

    18. I have control over my life

    19. I live the life that I desire

    20. My house is always prosperous

    21. Abundance is my portion

Motivation 4

    1. I am never alone

    2. I am strengthened in a mighty way

    3. I am very productive

    4. I have great strength because God's hand is upon me

    5. I can do great things

    6. I receive favor from people in high positions

    7. I am able to get others to cooperate

    8. I formulate excellent plans of action

    9. I actions help others

    10. I accomplish the assignments that come to me

Motivation 5

1. I am very wise
2. I always listen to good counsel
3. I take time to be still and meditate
4. I communicate from a place of love
5. I live in peace and safety
6. I quickly carry out my plans of action
7. I walk and live in prosperity
8. I am unique and because of that I am special
9. I am a seeker of truth and a follower of a right path
10. I am able to draw prosperity into this physical realm

NIGHTTIME

Night Hours

1. I enjoy deep peaceful sleep
2. My sleep is regenerative to my body
3. I see things from the now perspective
4. I receive excellent information during dreamtime
5. My actions bring prosperity to me
6. I make very exceptional plans to follow
7. I live and function in the present
8. Deep sleep helps me maintain a healthy body
9. My dreams are very valuable and instructional
10. I eagerly receive instructions in my night visions

TURNING INWARD

Turning Inward 1
1. Turning inward keeps abundance in my life
2. I turn inward to keep things running smoothly
3. I can turn inward for a fresh start
4. I find comfort when I turn inward
5. When I turn inward, I am able to find the answer to all things
6. My deliverance is found when I turn inward
7. My life is on track for success because I always turn inward
8. Turning inward empowers me to follow my right path
9. I turn inward to keep all areas of my life organized
10. Turning inward causes my feet to stand on solid ground

Turning Inward 2
1. I have strength when I turn inward
2. I am able to make my way straight by turning inward
3. I have stability when I turn inward
4. I am able to come to a place of prosperity by turning inward
5. I am safe and secure because I turn inward
6. I turn inward to God for every situation
7. I find everything that I need when I turn inward
8. I become calm and serene by turning inward
9. Turning inward opens up limitless possibilities for me
10. I find the God of my being when I turn inward

Victory

Victory 1

1. I excel quickly in all that I undertake
2. I make enormous progress in all of my endeavors
3. I am studious
4. I am victorious in all that I do
5. I speak fluently
6. Helpful information comes to me swiftly
7. The Universe listens when I speak
8. I receive all that I desire
9. I am very productive
10. I keep my eyes and mind focused

Victory 2

1. I meet every situation head-on
2. I am a problem solver
3. I have endurance and staying power
4. I can complete project in record time
5. I am very productive in my endeavors
6. I am optimistic
7. I take advantage of the many opportunities that come to me
8. People eagerly come to my aide and help me
9. I have an attitude of love and thankfulness which draw others to me
10. I rise above every situation

MIND/ THOUGHTS

Creative Thinking 1
1. I am creative in all that I do
2. I am very inventive
3. I am eternally resourceful
4. I formulate creative ideas easily and quickly
5. I give ideas freely to others
6. My creative mind is in sync with the creative forces of the universe
7. Ideas come to my mind frequently
8. My creative ideas bring prosperity to me
9. I am able to clearly express my creative ideas
10. My intuition helps my creativity

Creative Thinking 2
1. I act upon my creative ideas
2. Creative thoughts come to me naturally
3. I am tremendously imaginative in everything
4. The world is open to my creative ideas
5. I create ideas liberally
6. I allow creative ideas to freely flow through me
7. My creativity benefits myself and humanity
8. My mind produces creative artistic ideas
9. I experiment with my free thoughts
10. I am able to vocalize my ideas out loud

Creative Thinking 3

1. I am free to think creatively
2. I use my creative thoughts to find solutions
3. I spend time thinking about my creative ideas
4. I can think ahead of my time
5. I create artistic new things
6. I think positively
7. I welcome constructive criticism
8. I formulate ideas quickly and easily
9. I am only affected by my own opinions
10. I express myself freely

Creative Thinking

1. My creative thoughts grow daily
2. My thoughts evolve and expand my boundaries
3. I consider every question
4. My solutions are creative
5. I use my imagination daily
6. I am confident and sure in my thinking
7. I receive creative ideas freely
8. I am innovative
9. My creative thoughts brings prosperity to me
10. I enjoy creating

Memory 1

1. I remember everything I need to
2. I retain all necessary information

3. I have an excellent memory
4. I command my ability to remember events
5. I remember all of the information that I've received
6. I let memories come naturally
7. I absorb knowledge easily and freely
8. My outstanding memory serves me well
9. I share my memories wisely
10. I remember information accurately

Memory 2

1. I always remember things at will
2. I remember everything when I need to
3. My memory is powerful
4. I recall information easily and accurately
5. My memory is infinite
6. I use my memories to make informed decisions
7. I trust my memory completely
8. My memory improves everyday
9. I am calm when remembering things
10. I recall things quickly and accurately

Mind Power 1

1. My memory serves me well
2. I always recall the information I need
3. I always have perfect memory and recall
4. I recall and retain all of the information that I need to know
5. I use my memory effortlessly

6. I learn effortlessly and quickly
7. I am always focused and persistent
8. I read with comprehension
9. I listen intently
10. I am smart and energetic

Mind Power 2

1. I excel at tests and all of my undertakings
2. I remember quickly and easily
3. I am relaxed during tests
4. Answers come to me clearly
5. I have a powerful memory
6. Details are easy to remember and recall
7. Memory flows effortlessly
8. I am focused and I think clearly
9. My mental processes are sharp
10. I concentrate easily

Mind Power 3

1. I am good at all subjects
2. I am a logical thinker
3. My mind is keen
4. I am a genius
5. I am alert and focused
6. I am intuitive
7. I dream solutions
8. I am a quick thinker

9. I am insightful
10. I have a powerful vocabulary

Mind Power 4
1. I have an extensive vocabulary and I use words correctly
2. I speak well
3. I write well
4. I spell well
5. I imagine with all senses
6. Stimuli are sensory rich
7. I solve problems easily
8. Reading is easy for me
9. I read faster and faster
10. I read with great comprehension

Mind Power 5
1. I concentrate well when reading
2. I am a great reader
3. I learn quickly
4. I learn easily
5. I learn effortlessly
6. Every experience is an opportunity for success
7. Every experience is an opportunity for learning
8. I choose to learn
9. I use my learning wisely
10. I make wise choices

Mind Power 6

1. I recall the information I need whenever I need it
2. I have a perfect memory and recall
3. My brain is a wondrous storehouse of information
4. I can use my brain effortlessly
5. I am centered and focused
6. I am calm and alert
7. I am productive
8. I accomplish what I focus on
9. I see clearly
10. I am fluent in language

Reshaping thoughts 1

1. Every day in every way I move closer and closer to the true me.
2. I take action daily to improve myself.
3. I take action daily that shape my environment in a positive way.
4. I have full control over my thoughts and my actions.
5. My thoughts control my actions.
6. My thoughts are shaped by Universal truths.
7. The Universal Mind has deemed me successful.
8. My thoughts and my actions are positive and productive.
9. My truth is larger than the people that I meet or see.
10. My truth is greater than the experiences I have and see.

Reshaping thoughts 2

1. My truths come solely from the Universal Mind.
2. I only accept the truths of the Universal Mind.

3. I move with boldness and courage.
4. All of my actions produce beneficial results.
5. All of my thoughts are very productive for me.
6. I am free to think my own thoughts.
7. I am free to shape my environment by using my own thoughts.
8. I am free to be myself and express my inner desires.
9. I am free to bring my uniqueness to the world and live my dreams.
10. My unique qualities and attributes help the world in a positive way.
11. Only my opinion counts when it comes to how I see myself.

Super Memory 1
1. My brain is the world's best and most efficient super computer
2. My brain is supercharged and is always operating accurately
3. My thoughts are sharp and focused
4. I have lightening fast recall abilities
5. My ability to recall information is precise and very accurate
6. My brain possess an endless amount of energy
7. The neuro-transmitters and neuro-conductors in my brain are always firing
8. My brain has limitless potential
9. I recall thorough detailed information
10. My brain specializes in reasoning and recall

Super Memory 2
1. My brain logically and systematically recalls information
2. I am always able to recall information in detail
3. I get the proper rest and nutrition to power my brain
4. I drink large amounts of plain water help keep my brain operating efficiently
5. I am calm and confident when recalling information
6. It is easy and natural for me to store and recall information
7. All information in my brain is totally available to me
8. All the information that I have encountered or learn is stored in my brain
9. I can recall any and all of my brain's stored information
10. My brain gathers and stores information on a conscious and subconscious level

Super Memory 3
1. Information store in all levels of mind is available to me at will
2. I maintain my brain at a peak performance level
3. I consciously and subconsciously store information in my brain
4. My subconscious mind makes sure all useful information is stored in my brain
5. My brain functions like a well-oiled machine
6. I maintain positive thoughts to keep my brain moving in the right direction
7. All information in my brain is easy to access
8. I'm always in the habit of properly storing information in my brain

9. I take the time to commit information to memory
10. I recall information effortlessly

Super Memory 4
1. I articulate the information that I recall from my brain
2. I take full advantage of my brain's potential to store and recall information
3. My memory and recall is infinite
4. I always recall precise information
5. My brain quickly sorts and organizes the information that it takes in
6. I engage in exercises that sharpen my memory and recall abilities
7. I enjoy expanding my mind
8. My brain allows me to complete the projects that I start
9. I have total in depth recall of all information stored in my brain
10. I can quickly access detailed information

Thoughts 1
1. Every day in every way, I move closer and closer to the true me.
2. I take action daily to improve myself.
3. I take action daily that shape my environment in a positive way.
4. I have full control over my thoughts and my actions.
5. My thoughts control my actions.
6. My thoughts are shaped by Universal truths.
7. The Universal Mind has deemed me successful.
8. My thoughts and my actions are positive.
9. My truth is larger than the people that I meet or see.

10. My truth is greater than the experiences I have and see.

Thoughts 2
1. My truths come solely from the Universal Mind.
2. I only accept the truths of the Universal Mind.
3. I move with boldness and courage.
4. All of my actions produce beneficial results.
5. All of my thoughts are very productive for me.
6. I am free to think my own thoughts.
7. I am free to shape my environment by using my own thoughts.
8. I am free to be myself and express my inner desires.
9. I am free to bring my uniqueness to the world and live my dreams.
10. My unique qualities and attributes help the world in a positive way.
11. Only my opinion counts when it comes to how I see myself.

MONEY

Millionaire Mind 1
1. I think positive thoughts
2. I consider only positive suggestions
3. I am influenced by positive thoughts and suggestions
4. I live day by day in excellent health
5. I am surrounded by wealth

6. I have unlimited wealth
7. I enjoy excellent health, wealth, and happiness
8. I am at one with Universal Mind
9. My thoughts generate enormous amounts of wealth and prosperity
10. My brainwaves are tuned to natural success frequencies

Millionaire Mind 2

1. My energy generates wealth, success, and prosperity
2. I am only receptive to ideas and situations beneficial to me
3. Only beneficial conditions and circumstances happen to me
4. It is my Universal right to be wealthy
5. I live in Divine health
6. I live and move in Divine wealth
7. Wealth flows to me naturally
8. My mind is alert to financial opportunities
9. I receive opportunities to enhance my financial standing
10. I have highly effective methods that draw wealth to me

Millionaire Mind 3

1. My ideas and thoughts generate perpetual wealth
2. I am able to brainstorm at a moments notice
3. I conduct meetings that generate wealth
4. I am very insightful, modern, and up to date
5. I am very knowledgeable about technology
6. I am extremely original and inventive
7. I am a technology expert

8. My thoughts are magnets for wealth
9. I attract large sums of wealth to me
10. My actions attract wealth

Millionaire Mind 4

1. I am a mover and a shaker
2. I actions and idea multiple my wealth daily
3. I freely exchange money to create a circuit for wealth to come back to me
4. I emit vibrations, thoughts, and energy that draw wealth, health, and prosperity to me
5. I attract money like honey attracts bees
6. There is a constant flow of wealth into my life
7. I constantly attract enormous amounts of wealth
8. I am a wealth magnet
9. I attract wealth with every thought and idea
10. I vibrate to the frequency of wealth

Millionaire Mind 5

1. I enjoy money and what money does for me
2. Money is constantly flowing and circulating in my life
3. Money loves to work for me
4. I turn money into wealth
5. Everything about me expresses wealth
6. Wealth loves being with me
7. I know how to multiply the wealth that comes to me
8. I use wealth wisely and effectively

9. I use wealth for expansion
10. Wealth is allowed to flow to me and circulate in my environment

Millionaire Mind 6

1. I have a positive attitude concerning wealth
2. I am thorough and efficient in the affairs concerning wealth
3. I am experienced in handling large amounts of wealth
4. I use my wealth to bring about positive change
5. I conduct highly profitable negotiations with money
6. I have very profitable moneymaking ideas
7. My business grows exponentially everyday
8. My services and sales bring increase to me
9. I have highly effective wealth generating plans
10. I see situations from every angle

Millionaire Mind 7

1. I turn every situation and circumstance into a profitable one
2. The Universe constantly brings wealth to me
3. I manifest wealth in every area of my life
4. I am well versed in language
5. I express myself and my thoughts well
6. I am articulate and very decisive
7. I function very well in all arenas
8. I am direct, to the point and tactful
9. I network with productive people
10. I am very punctual and make wise use of my time

Millionaire Mind 8

1. I am well groomed, stylish, and professional in appearance
2. I handle large sums of wealth daily
3. I only deal with matters of importance
4. I am a mogul in handling and dealing with wealth
5. I am wise in business dealings and money matters
6. I am well able to handle and take control in all situations
7. My mind is sharp and I am a quick thinker
8. I turn time into money and money into wealth
9. I see the positive aspect of all things and all situations
10. I always have the advantage and the upper hand in all situations

Millionaire Mind 9

1. Events and circumstances turn out in my favor
2. I am the master of my destiny
3. I turn every situation into a winning one
4. I am a prominent figure that possess an excellent character
5. I set examples for others to follow
6. Wealth building opportunities come to me daily
7. My life has meaningful purpose and I make the most of everyday
8. I live a very productive and prosperous life
9. I am an excellent leader and I set a positive example for others to follow
10. My lifestyle breeds wealth

Millionaire Mind 10

1. The world is open to me
2. Wealth comes to me on many levels
3. I have multiple streams of revenue
4. I am a self-starter and a trendsetter
5. I am always prepare
6. I have a value sound plan for prosperity
7. I am organized and have a knack for handling situations successfully
8. I develop a system for handling everything
9. I have an extremely high success rate
10. I have favor with the Universe and with others

Money 1

1. I have right relationship with money
2. I am an heir to all of the money in the universe
3. I keep money circulating in my life
4. I make very wise decisions concerning money
5. The money I circulate is planted in the etheric and spiritual realms of the universe
6. I have an excellent ongoing relationship with money
7. I am the best power-player in matters concerning money
8. I am a powerful money magnet
9. Large sums of money comes to me quickly and easily
10. Money is constantly rushing to be with me

Money 2
1. Money is always finding a way to come under my control
2. Money comes into my hands as I go out and as I come in
3. Each drop of dew gently rehydrates the seeds of money that I plant
4. All of the money that I circulate comes back to me multiplied by 30 times, 70 times, or 100 times
5. Every drop of rain waters my action of prosperity or money producing actions
6. Each ray of the sun brings a harvest of money to me
7. Money is always readily available to me
8. Money grows on trees and springs up out of the ground for me
9. I am thoroughly trained in the art of making money
10. I have the money of the universe at my disposal

Money 3
1. Money falls into my lap like leaves falling off a tree
2. My money increases daily by leaps and bounds
3. I make the most of every moment and every moment is a money making moment
4. My moneymaking thoughts are always beneficial for me
5. I have the power to obtain large sums of money
6. The money I plant always goes into enriched fertile ground and brings a bountiful harvest to me
7. I develop partnerships that bring me money
8. I create money in my waking state and during my dream state
9. My money attracts even more money to me

10. Money always comes to me easily and quickly
11. Large sums of money come to me in steady streams

Money Magnet 1
1. I make wise decisions concerning money
2. I am thrifty and wise when spending money
3. I am in full control of all aspects of my money
4. I save large amounts of money regularly
5. I expect great prosperity
6. Money comes to me quick, fast, and in a hurry
7. I earn large sums of money effortlessly
8. I have a continual flow of money coming to me
9. I have access to large amounts of money
10. I am a powerful money magnet

Money Magnet 2
1. I have a responsible plan concerning money matters
2. I constantly receive large sums of money
3. Money comes to me in miraculous ways
4. I am open to receiving abundant wealth
5. Money beats a path to my door
6. The Universe sends enormous amounts of money to me
7. My thoughts attract money in constant streams
8. Money constantly searches me out
9. I use debt to attract money
10. I am always wise about money matters

Money Magnet 3
1. I easily manage my finances
2. Large sums of money constantly come to me
3. I am relaxed concerning finances
4. It's okay to be wealthy and happy
5. My joy attracts financial resources
6. Money Angels work to bring constant flows of money to me
7. I am constantly adding to my income
8. I live with an abundance of wealth
9. My time brings large sums of money to me
10. I have more than enough money

Money Magnet 4
1. Everything I touch quickly returns riches to me
2. Dealing with money is as easy as breathing
3. I recognize good workable moneymaking ventures
4. My actions bring large sums of money to me
5. I have hidden money resources that are easily and readily accessible to me
6. Everything about me attracts enormous amounts of money
7. I plant seeds that bring large financial harvests of money to me
8. I have an air about me that attracts money
9. I enjoy attracting money and being wealthy
10. Large sums of money constantly race to me in steady streams

Wealth 1

1. I have right relationship with wealth
2. I am an heir to all of the wealth in the universe
3. I keep wealth circulating in my life
4. I make very wise decisions concerning wealth
5. The wealth I circulate is planted in the etheric and spiritual realms of the universe
6. I have an excellent ongoing relationship with wealth
7. I am a power-player in matters concerning wealth
8. I am a wealth magnet
9. Large sums of wealth come to me quickly and easily
10. Wealth is constantly rushing to be with me

Wealth 2

1. Wealth is always finding a way to come into my hands and under my control
2. Wealth comes into my hands as I go out and as I come in
3. Each drop of dew gently rehydrates the seeds of wealth that I plant
4. All of the wealth that I circulate comes back to me multiplied by 30 times, 70 times, or 100 times
5. Every drop of rain waters my actions of prosperity or wealth producing actions
6. Each ray of the sun brings a harvest of wealth to me
7. Wealth is always readily available to me
8. Wealth grows on trees and springs up out of the ground for me
9. I am thoroughly trained in the art of obtaining wealth

10. I have all of the wealth of the universe at my disposal

Wealth 3
1. Enormous amounts of wealth fall into my lap like leaves falling off a tree
2. My wealth increases daily by leaps and bounds
3. I make the most of every moment and every moment is a wealth making moment
4. My wealth making thoughts are always beneficial for me
5. I have the power to obtain large sums of wealth
6. The wealth I plant always goes into enriched fertile ground and brings a bountiful harvest to me
7. I develop partnerships that bring me wealth
8. I create wealth in my waking state and during my dream state
9. My wealth attracts even more wealth to me
10. Wealth always comes to me easily and quickly
11. Large sums of wealth come to me in steady streams

RELEASING

Releasing 1
1. I release thoughts that hinder my progress.
2. I release and let go of habits that slow my performance.
3. I release and rid myself of beliefs that are counterproductive to me.

4. I rid myself of limitations
5. I move and live in the present
6. I release unproductive habits
7. I release people that maybe hindering my progress
8. I quickly release stress and tension
9. I release hurtful thoughts and situations
10. I release people from my life that are unsupportive

Releasing 2

1. I release unproductive thoughts
2. I decide what I keep
3. I move with a positive attitude
4. I learn from my past
5. I let my past experiences go when they no longer server my best interests
6. I am free from unwanted memories
7. I quickly release memories that are not helpful
8. I define myself
9. I maintain a positive state of mind
10. I live only in the present

Releasing 3

1. I appreciate my past as a learning tool
2. I accept the decisions I have made
3. I make decisions I am happy with
4. I make decisions that are most helpful to me
5. I control my memories and thoughts

6. I let go of all regrets
7. I am free to live in the present
8. I am the pilot of my mind, memories, and thoughts
9. I understand people can change over time
10. My past is only my past

Releasing 4

1. My present state of mind has power over everything
2. I share my memories wisely
3. I plan my future using past experiences
4. I only keep happy memories
5. I release all grudges
6. I feel good forgiving people
7. I think about the present and the future
8. I live in the present
9. I am free to move with positive actions
10. I release all unwanted memories and unwanted thoughts

SLEEP/ DREAM

Lucid Dreaming 1

1. I know when I'm dreaming
2. I am fully aware in my sleep
3. I remember my dreams vividly

4. I control my dreams
5. I easily control the events in my dreams
6. I ask myself if I am dreaming
7. My dreams provides vital and helpful information
8. I am receptive to the information that comes through my dreams
9. My dreams are very important
10. I look forward to my dream state and what it brings to me

Lucid Dreaming 2

1. My dreams are very vivid
2. I do amazing things when I dream
3. I am able to have fascinating experiences while dreaming
4. Important information comes to me through my dreams
5. My dreams provide unlimited experiences and opportunities
6. My dreams give me a unique platform
7. I make good use of the information that comes through my dreams
8. I quickly take control of my dreams
9. I instantly recognize when I am dreaming
10. I know when I am asleep

Lucid Dreaming 3

1. I am conscious when I dream
2. I remember the events of my dreams
3. I know I can do anything when I dream
4. I know I can create or destroy anything in my dreams
5. I know when I am dreaming

6. I live my fantasies in my dreams
7. I solve my problems through my dreams
8. My dreams are clear and crisp
9. I am in full control of my dreams
10. I am invincible in my dreams

Lucid Dreaming 4

1. I am anything I want to be in my dreams
2. I know when I am sleeping
3. The information I receive from dreams is very useful
4. I welcome my dreams
5. I can control all aspects of my dreams
6. I can obtain hidden information from my dreams
7. I go anywhere in my dreams
8. I can do anything in my dreams
9. I wake up from my dream state when I want to
10. I remember my dreams easily and completely

Sleep time 1

1. Sleep comes to me effortlessly
2. I set aside the day's activities when it's time for sleep
3. I quickly fall into a deep sleep
4. My sleep is always sound, peaceful, and restful
5. I am healthy because I get a good night's sleep
6. My sleep restores my energy
7. Being well rested helps me achieve success

8. My body is rejuvenate because I always achieve a state of deep sleep
9. My body heals and restores itself during my deep sleep state
10. I reflect favorably on my daily accomplishments

Sleep time 2
1. I relax quickly and fall into a deep deep sleep
2. I am able to resolve lingering issues during my nightly dream state
3. My nightly sleep allows me to awake refreshed and energetic
4. I start each day fresh and with vigor
5. I enjoy a deep restful sleep
6. I go through each day with ease because I get good sleep
7. I handle daily events and situations with ease because I am well rested
8. I always have a restful and peaceful sleep time
9. I am very productive because I get good sleep
10. I take full advantage of opportunities because I am fully rested

SPEAKING

Public Speaking 1
1. My public speaking flows naturally
2. I deliver speeches with admirable skill
3. My knowledge flows easily when speaking
4. I dress professionally during speaking engagements

5. I have full confidence when speaking
6. I enjoy public speaking
7. I love sharing information through public speaking
8. I develop my points clearly and completely
9. I am very eloquent and fluent when speaking
10. I always make eye contact with my audience
11. I deal with distractions professionally

Public Speaking 2

1. I am a very helpful and informative speaker
2. I keep my mind and thoughts focused during a speech
3. My speeches are exciting and expressive
4. I think only about the information specific to the speech that I'm giving
5. I hold the attention of every person in my audience
6. I remember all portions of my speeches accurately
7. I use my speeches to fully express my wisdom and to pass on information
8. I am a natural born speaker
9. I present myself and my information in a professional manner
10. I accurately interpret the audience's body language
11. I deliver helpful and informative information to my audience

Public Speaking 3

1. It is like second nature for me when I speak in public
2. I speak respectfully to others
3. I use wit to keep the audience laughing

4. I always have the full attention of the audience
5. I explain my points clearly and completely
6. I deliver clear, accurate, and detailed information
7. I make my words flow in order
8. I deliver my information with precision and accuracy
9. I pronounce my words clearly and distinctly
10. I use body language to add flair
11. I am completely calm when speaking

SUCCESS

Reshaping for Success 1

1. Only my opinion matters when it comes to my ability to succeed
2. I see myself as very talented and very successful
3. The universe works with me to create great success
4. I take joy in setting positive goals for myself
5. I easily accomplish the goals that I set
6. I am able to easily access my hidden potential
7. I am open to new positive ideas that will bring me success
8. I only entertain positive winning thoughts
9. I make great use of my time
10. All of my thoughts are positive and bring me great success

Reshaping for Success 2

1. I plan my day in a manner that will bring me success

2. My mind is full of positive successful thoughts
3. I am able to come up with a successful plan for every situation that I face
4. I make positive successful contacts throughout each day
5. The Universe works continuously to bring me great success
6. I make powerful moves each day that bring me great success
7. Success comes to me easily and swiftly
8. I enjoy working towards my goals
9. I work from a happy peace filled place
10. I am successful in all that I do

Success 1
1. Every day in every way, I become more and more successful.
2. Only my opinion matters when it comes to my ability to succeed.
3. I see myself as very talented and very successful.
4. The universe works with me to create great success.
5. I take joy in setting positive goals for myself.
6. I easily accomplish the goals that I set.
7. I am able to easily access my hidden potential.
8. I am open to new positive ideas that will bring me success.
9. I only entertain positive winning thoughts.
10. I make great use of my time.

Success 2
1. All of my thoughts are positive and bring me great success.
2. I plan my day in a manner that will bring me success.
3. My mind is full of positive successful thoughts.

4. I am able to come up with a successful plan for every situation that I face.
5. I make positive successful contacts throughout each day.
6. The Universe works continuously to bring me great success.
7. I make powerful moves each day that bring me great success.
8. Success comes to me easily and swiftly.
9. I work from a happy peace filled place.
10. I am successful in all that I do.

Success 3

1. I enjoy working towards my goals.
2. All that I do works together to help me reach my goals.
3. I enjoy working because it causes me to reach my goals.
4. I obtain success in all of my endeavors.
5. I am successful in all that I do.
6. Success has always been part of my life.
7. I enjoy a wealth of success.
8. I enjoy all that success brings
9. I'm fully aware of what will move me into success.
10. My actions always lead to success.

Success 4

1. I mentally, emotionally, and physically move to success.
2. I move with precision to achieve success.
3. I feel wonderful because I live in success.
4. I am invigorated and fully energized and able to maintain success in all areas of my life.

5. I live life in the fullness of success.
6. Day by day in every way, I move and live in great success.
7. I am naturally successful
8. It is very easy for me to maintain success
9. Reaching the positive goals that I set for myself has made me successful
10. I have a successful and rewarding life

PROSPERITY

Prosperity
1. I open myself up to receive fresh positive ideas
2. I allow myself to come into events and information that will enhance my life
3. I always receive information that will cause me to greatly prosper
4. I open myself up to the wellspring of the universe
5. I enjoy health, wealth, and prosperity
6. I am vibrant and productive
7. Good things always come to me
8. I rest in the knowledge that great things await me at every turn
9. Everyday and in every way I live a successful and joy filled life
10. Everything in my environment gets better and better.

WEIGHT

Weight loss 1

1. I am always at my ideal weight
2. I enjoy being slender
3. I maintain a healthy body
4. I enjoy small quantities of lean meat
5. My appetite is easily satisfied
6. I eat small size portions of food
7. I enjoy my food when I eat it
8. Small size portions of food is very satisfying and filling
9. I eat to maintain a healthy body
10. I enjoy the taste and flavor of my food

Weight loss 2

1. I only eat to nourish my body
2. The food that I eat helps to keep me healthy
3. I enjoy eating plenty of fresh vegetables
4. I eat food to build a strong healthy body
5. I eat foods that are high in vitamins and minerals
6. I eat foods that boost my metabolism
7. I develop lean tone muscular structure
8. My food is always lean and nutritious
9. My body utilizes its stored energy deposits
10. My energy level and metabolism is always steady and high

Weight loss 3

1. I only crave healthy nutritious foods
2. I enjoy exercises and activities that keep me physically healthy
3. I only eat the amount of food needed to maintain a healthy body
4. My food is prepared using only healthy seasonings and methods
5. I always eat in moderation
6. I eat leafy green vegetables that are high in nutrition
7. My taste and cravings are only for the things my body needs
8. I eat my food slowly
9. I take small bites when eating
10. I chew my food completely

Weight loss 4

1. I get pleasure from eating only the nutritional foods that my body needs
2. My food digests quickly and efficiently
3. I like eating fresh foods and vegetables
4. I enjoy activities that keep me physically healthy
5. I eat healthy nuts, fruits, and vegetables
6. My body only retains the nutrients that it needs to operate efficiently
7. My body only needs small portions and quantities of food
8. I feel and look better because I eat healthy
9. Being healthy makes me stronger and more energetic
10. I subconsciously know what foods my body needs

Weight loss 5

1. My subconscious mind controls my appetite
2. My body reacts in a positive manner with healthy foods
3. I only eat the foods that my body requires
4. I efficiently use the stored reserves of energy from my entire body
5. My daily activities uses enormous amount of energy
6. Everyday I grow stronger and healthier
7. I exercise to maintain my healthy body
8. My body's measurements and weight matches my bone structure
9. My body measurements and weight is in accordance with healthy standards
10. I feel healthy and strong everyday

Section 6
Color Scripts C

Aquamarine

I'll find myself emerging from my resting state, feeling happy, feeling proud, feeling elated that I am successful and prosperous in all that I do. I realize that I have found a way to easily access and utilize my greatest resources. Each and every time I see the color AQUAMARINE, whether consciously or unconsciously, my desire and determination to succeed will grow stronger. Each and every suggestion received in this session will work more and more effectively. I will not need to look for the color aquamarine, but I will just notice it automatically. It will be bright, sharp, and clear to me. Each and every suggestion I have received here in this session will continue to work more and more effectively every time I see the color AQUAMARINE... AQUAMARINE... AQUAMARINE.

Black

I'll find myself emerging from my resting state, feeling happy, feeling proud, feeling elated that I am successful and prosperous in all that I do. I realize that I have found a way to easily access and utilize my greatest

resources. Each and every time I see the color BLACK, whether consciously or subconsciously, my desire and determination to succeed will grow stronger. Each and every suggestion received in this session will work more and more effectively. I will not need to look for the color black, but I will just notice it automatically. It will be bright, sharp, and clear to me. Each and every suggestion I have received here in this session will continue to work more and more effectively every time I see the color BLACK…BLACK…BLACK.

Blue

I will find myself emerging from my resting state, feeling happy, feeling proud, feeling elated that I am successful and prosperous in all that I do. I realize that I have found a way to easily access and utilize my greatest resources. Each and every time I see the color BLUE, whether consciously or subconsciously, my desire and determination to succeed will grow stronger. Each and every suggestion received in this session will work more and more effectively. I will not need to look for the color blue, but I will notice it automatically. It will be bright, sharp, and clear to me.

Brown

I'll find myself emerging from my resting state, feeling happy, feeling proud, feeling elated that I am successful and prosperous in all that I do. I realize that I have found a way to easily access and utilize my greatest resources. Each and every time I see the color BROWN, whether consciously or unconsciously, my desire and determination to succeed will grow stronger. Each and every suggestion received in this session will work more and more effectively. I will not need to look for the color brown, but I will just notice it automatically. It will be bright, sharp, and clear to me. Each and every suggestion I have received here in this session will continue to work more and more effectively every time I see the color BROWN...BROWN...BROWN.

Fuchsia

I'll find myself emerging from my resting state, feeling happy, feeling proud, feeling elated that I am successful and prosperous in all that I do. I realize that I have found a way to easily access and utilize my greatest resources. Each and every time I see the color FUSHIA, whether consciously or subconsciously, my desire and determination to succeed will grow stronger. Each and every suggestion received in this session will work more and more effectively. I will not need to look for the color fuchsia, but I will just notice it automatically. It will be bright, sharp, and clear to me. Each and every suggestion I have received here in this session will continue to work more and more effectively every time I see the color FUSHIA...FUSHIA...FUSHIA.

Gold

I'll find myself emerging from my resting state, feeling happy, feeling proud, feeling elated that I am successful and prosperous in all that I do. I realize that I have found a way to easily access and utilize my greatest resources. Each and every time I see the color GOLD, whether consciously or subconsciously, my desire and determination to succeed will grow stronger. Each and every suggestion received in this session will work more and more effectively. I will not need to look for the color gold, but I will just notice it automatically. It will be bright, sharp, and clear to me. Each and every suggestion I have received here in this session will continue to work more and more effectively every time I see the color GOLD…GOLD…GOLD.

Green

I'll find myself emerging from my resting state, feeling happy, feeling proud, feeling elated that I am successful and prosperous in all that I do. I realize that I have found a way to easily access and utilize my greatest resources. Each and every time I see the color GREEN, whether consciously or subconsciously, my desire and determination to succeed will grow stronger. Each and every suggestion received in this session will work more and more effectively. I will not need to look for the color green, but I will just notice it automatically. It will be bright, sharp, and clear to me. Each and every suggestion I have received here in this session will continue to work more and more effectively every time I see the color GREEN…GREEN…GREEN.

Grey

I'll find myself emerging from my resting state, feeling happy, feeling proud, feeling elated that I am successful and prosperous in all that I do. I realize that I have found a way to easily access and utilize my greatest

resources. Each and every time I see the color GREY, whether consciously or subconsciously, my desire and determination to succeed will grow stronger. Each and every suggestion received in this session will work more and more effectively. I will not need to look for the color grey, but I will just notice it automatically. It will be bright, sharp, and clear to me. Each and every suggestion I have received here in this session will continue to work more and more effectively every time I see the color GREY...GREY...GREY.

Orange

I'll find myself emerging from my resting state, feeling happy, feeling proud, feeling elated that I am successful and prosperous in all that I do. I realize that I have found a way to easily access and utilize my greatest resources. Each and every time I see the color ORANGE, whether consciously or subconsciously, my desire and determination to succeed will grow stronger. Each and every suggestion received in this session will work more and more effectively. I will not need to look for the color orange, but I will just notice it automatically. It will be bright, sharp, and clear to me. Each and every suggestion I have received here in this session will continue to work more and more effectively every time I see the color ORANGE...ORANGE...ORANGE.

Pink

I'll find myself emerging from my resting state, feeling happy, feeling proud, feeling elated that I am successful and prosperous in all that I do. I realize that I have found a way to easily access and utilize my greatest

resources. Each and every suggestion I have received here in this session will continue to work more and more effectively every time I see the color PINK...PINK...PINK.

Purple

I'll find myself emerging from my resting state, feeling happy, feeling proud, feeling elated that I am successful and prosperous in all that I do. I realize that I have found a way to easily access and utilize my greatest resources. Each and every suggestion I have received here in this session will continue to work more and more effectively every time I see the color PURPLE...PURPLE...PURPLE.

Red

I'll find myself emerging from my resting state, feeling happy, feeling proud, feeling elated that I am successful and prosperous in all that I do. I realize that I have found a way to easily access and utilize my greatest resources. Each and every suggestion I have received here in this session will continue to work more and more effectively every time I see the color RED...RED...RED.

Silver

I'll find myself emerging from my resting state, feeling happy, feeling proud, feeling elated that I am successful and prosperous in all that I do. I realize that I have found a way to easily access and utilize my greatest resources. Each and every suggestion I have received here in this session will continue to work more and more effectively every time I see the color SILVER...SILVER...SILVER.

Turquoise

I'll find myself emerging from my resting state, feeling happy, feeling proud, feeling elated that I am successful and prosperous in all that I do. I realize that I have found a way to easily access and utilize my greatest resources. Each and every suggestion I have received here in this session will continue to work more and more effectively every time I see the color TURQUOISE...TURQUOISE...TURQUOISE.

Violet

I'll find myself emerging from my resting state, feeling happy, feeling proud, feeling elated that I am successful and prosperous in all that I do. I realize that I have found a way to easily access and utilize my greatest resources. Each and every suggestion I have received here in this session will continue to work more and more effectively every time I see the color VIOLET...VIOLET...VIOLET.

White

I'll find myself emerging from my resting state, feeling happy, feeling proud, feeling elated that I am successful and prosperous in all that I do. I realize that I have found a way to easily access and utilize my greatest resources. Each and every suggestion I have received here in this session will continue to work more and more effectively every time I see the color WHITE...WHITE...WHITE.

Yellow

I'll find myself emerging from my resting state, feeling happy, feeling proud, feeling elated that I am successful and prosperous in all that I do. I realize that I have found a way to easily access and utilize my greatest resources. Each and every suggestion I have received here in this session will continue to work more and more effectively every time I see the color YELLOW…YELLOW…YELLOW.

Section 7
Closers

Power Play Closer

> Power Play Closer is used when making scripts to be used at anytime of the day except sleeping. These are great for daily commutes, at lunch/break times, etc.

I direct the flow of thoughts allowing my subconscious mind to take in all that is suggested and then act on it to bring me into greater prosperity and success.

Each and every time I listen to this, it will be 10 times more effective in helping me reach my goals successfully.

Awake Closer

> Awake Closer is used when making scripts that will be used at time of the day that permit quiet time, meditation times, or down time. **Never use this in a Power Play Script.**

I will now count from 1 to 5 and return to a normal fully attentive conscious state.

1 - All suggestions have been planted deep within my subconscious mind and will have an immediate positive effect on my life.

2 – Once I return to a conscious state I will be fully alert, completely relaxed, at ease, energized, and ready for the day.

3 - My conscious and subconscious mind quickly works hand in hand to keep me in a lifestyle that I desire.

4 - Each time I listen to this, it will be 10 times more effective in helping me reach my goals successfully.

5 - I am refreshed, fully conscious, energized, relaxed, and at ease.

Sleep Closer

> Sleep Closer is used only when making scripts that will be used at night or when you're going to sleep. **Never use in a Power Script.**

I will now drift off to sleep, sleeping deeply and comfortably. Enjoying the most restful sleep that I can imagine. My suggestions will have been planted deep within my subconscious mind and will have an immediate positive effect on my life. My conscious and subconscious mind quickly works hand in hand to keep me in a lifestyle that I desire. When I awake at my usual time, I will wake up fully alert, completely relaxed, at ease, energized, and ready for the day.

Each time I listen to this, it will be 10 times more effective in helping me reach my goals successfully.

APPENDIX

Recording Templates:

POWER PLAY	
Script Part	Section
Power Play Opener	1
Trigger Color A	2
Suggestions	5
Trigger Color B	4
Power Play Closer	7
Please note section number 4 &5 are not in order	

AWAKE	
Script Part	Section
Awake Opener	1
Trigger Color A	2
Induction	3
Trigger Color B	4
Suggestions	5
Trigger Color C	6
Awake Closer	7
Only use the Opener &Closer labeled for Awake in these recordings	

SLEEP	
Script Part	Section
Sleep Opener	1
Trigger Color A	2
Induction	3
Trigger Color B	4
Suggestions	5
Trigger Color C	6
Sleep Closer	7
Only use the Opener &Closer labeled for Sleep in these recordings	

INDEX

A

Advisor, 163
Anchors, 68
Aquamarine, 81, 127, 205
Avoid, 39
Awake, 61, 62, 67, 68, 73, 213, 217

B

Background, 66, 72
Balance, 19
Black, 81, 127, 205
Blanket, 94
Blue, 81, 127, 206
Breath, 95
Brown, 82, 128, 206
Business, 133, 134, 137, 138

C

Candle, 87
Commands, 34
Confidence, 140, 141, 142, 143, 144, 145, 146, 147
Creative, 172, 173
Creativity, 148, 149
Criticism, 150
Crystal, 91

D

Decisions, 151, 152
Desires, 153, 154
Dolphin, 92
Dreaming, 193, 194, 195
Dreamtime, 92

E

Einstein, 17
Energy, 17, 154, 155
Exam, 156, 157, 158, 159

F

Fuchsia, 82, 128, 207

G

Garden, 107, 112, 121
Goals, 24, 160, 161
Gold, 82, 128, 207
Green, 83, 129, 208
Grey, 83, 129, 208

H

Health, 161, 162

I

Inner, 163
Inward, 170
Island, 122

J

Job, 164, 165, 166

L

Lazy, 99
Lucid, 193, 194, 195

M

Magnet, 188, 189
Memory, 173, 174, 175, 178, 179, 180
Millionaire, 181, 182, 183, 184, 185, 186
Mind, 44, 148, 159, 174, 175, 176, 177, 180, 181, 182, 183, 184, 185, 186
Money, 3, 5, 6, 11, 41, 42, 138, 183, 186, 187, 188, 189
Motivation, 144, 164, 165, 166, 167, 168, 169

N

Night, 107, 113, 169
NLP, 15, 70

O

Orange, 83, 129, 209
Oriented, 134, 135, 136

P

Paradise, 117
Pink, 84, 130, 209
Pool, 100
Power, 56, 60, 61, 67, 68, 73, 77, 138, 139, 140, 174, 175, 176, 177, 213, 217
Power Play, 56, 61, 67, 68, 73, 77, 213, 217
Prioritizing, 11, 27
Private, 105, 107
Product, 134, 135
Programming, 70
Prosperity, 3, 5, 6, 11, 47, 48, 49, 201
Purple, 84, 130, 210

R

Real Estate, 11, 23
Red, 84, 92, 130, 210
Relaxed, 109, 110, 114
Releasing, 191, 192, 193
Reshaping, 177, 198

S

Scenario, 28, 29, 30

Secret, 112
Self-Hypnosis, 5, 6, 58
Selling, 138, 139, 140
Service, 135, 136
Silver, 85, 131, 210
Sleep, 58, 61, 62, 67, 68, 73, 195, 196, 214, 218
Speaking, 196, 197
Staircase, 125
Steps, 119
Success, 11, 37, 137, 138, 198, 199, 200
Swimming, 117

T

Templates, 217
Thoughts, 180, 181
Triggers, 68, 69
Turquoise, 85, 131, 211

V

Victory, 171
Violet, 85, 131, 211
Volume, 57

W

Wealth, 3, 5, 6, 11, 43, 44, 45, 46, 182, 183, 184, 185, 186, 190, 191
Weight, 202, 203, 204
White, 86, 132, 211

Y

Yellow, 86, 132, 212

www.money-wealthandprosperity.com

MP3 Recordings

Our MP3s are like having your very own motivational coach whenever you need. These recordings will help to focus your mind and give direction to your thoughts. They help to weed out information that is of no use to you thereby allowing you to refocus your thoughts. Our recordings help you quickly and easily make necessary changes so that you are continuously moving towards your goals.

The information contained on our recordings goes directly into the super conscious part of your bran in a manner that provides the best possible results in the shortest amount of time. You are able to rid yourself of unproductive thoughts and actions that hinder your progress. You are able to no only change the direction of your thoughts but to give them a new focus and aim. This is done by weeding out thoughts that are not longer useful. The recordings also weed out blocks of information that are counterproductive to your goals.

Our MP3 recordings help you focus your mind and maintain that focus so that your thoughts and actions continually move you towards your goals. We are upfront concerning the information that we use in our recordings. We use NLP and hypnotic techniques to help you achieve your goals. We present a clean recording so there is nothing hidden. You are relaxed, at ease, and able to use the information presented without reservation.

Our MP3s Contain:
NO *Masking*
NO *Hidden messages*
NO *Manipulative sounds*
NO *Manipulative suggestions*
NO *Tricks*

Visit us online: www.money-wealthandprosperity.com

www.money-wealthandprosperity.com

Specialty Cards

These little cards are packed with powerful words that help you in reaching your goals. They mimic our MP3 suggestions and work to reinforce that which your motivational coach has stated. Our Specialty Cards truly inspire and help to keep you focused on where you are going or what you desire to achieve.

These special little cards are available in easy to carry business card sizes that can be kept in your wallet, rolodex, card file, or purse for easy access. They are also available as magnets to post on your refrigerator, desk, locker, file cabinet, or other metal surface.

Bite size easy to digest nuggets that you can use throughout the day. Keep these at your fingertips to cheer you onwards to your desired goals. They help you maintain a "You can do it" attitude.

Visit us online: www.money-wealthandprosperity.com

www.ingramcontent.com/pod-product-compliance
Lightning Source LLC
Chambersburg PA
CBHW050557170426
43201CB00011B/1732